Science Textbook
Year 5–6

Series Editor: Alan Jarvis

Joan O'Sullivan
Ian Baldry
Andrew Hodges
William Merrick
Pat Szczesniak

Letts
EDUCATIONAL

Every effort has been made to trace copyright holders and to obtain their permission for the use of copyright material. The authors and publishers would gladly receive information enabling them to rectify any error or omission in subsequent editions.

Photographic credits
Dr Rod Preston-Mafham/Premaphotos Wildlife: 11 (topleft, topright); Robert Battersby/Bosun: 18, 22, 41, 63, 64, 80, 81 (top, bottom), 93, 98 (top), 99 (top, bottom), 126 (top, bottom), 127, 140 (top, bottom); Sautelet, Jerrican/Science Photo Library: 26; Sally Morgan/ Ecoscene: 36; Robin Scargill/Galaxy: 89; Allan Morton/Science Photo Library: 90; John Sanford/Science Photo Library: 91 (top); NASA/Science Photo Library: 91 (bottom); Mark N. Boulton/ICCE: 98 (bottom); George Bernard/Science Photo Library: 102; Graham Buchan/Lifefile: 103; Andrew Lambert: 107 (left, centre, right), 109 (left, centre, right).

First published 1998
10 9

Letts Educational,
The Chiswick Centre
414 Chiswick High Road,
London W4 5TF
Tel: 0845 602 1937
Fax: 020 8742 8767

Text © Ian Baldry, Andrew Hodges, Alan Jarvis, William Merrick, Joan O'Sullivan, Pat Szczesniak

Designed, edited and produced by Gecko Limited, Cambridge

Illustrations by Brett Breckon, Helen Humphreys, Margaret Jones, John Plumb, Chris Rothero and Janet Simmonett

Picture research by Lodestone Publishing Ltd
Cover photographs supplied by Educational Solutions, 49 Jessop Court, Ferry Street, Bristol BS1 6HP.

British Library Cataloguing-in-Publication Data
A CIP record for this book is available from the British Library

ISBN 1 84085 062 0

Printed in UK

Letts Educational Limited is a division of Granada Learning Limited, part of Granada plc.

Contents

How do I get the best out of this book?

How is the book organised?

The **contents page** near the front of the book shows you the topics in each unit.

I look at the contents page to find where something is in the book.

Each unit has a different colour to make it easier to find. For example, 'Keeping healthy' is blue.

There are **nine units** in the book. Each unit is organised in the same way. They have:

Before I start a new topic I look at the first page of the unit. This helps me to think about what I need to know before I start a topic.

- an **introduction page** – The top part of this page tells you what you should already know. Use this to check what you can remember about each topic. If there is something you don't know, you will have to do some catching up. The bottom part of the page shows you what you will learn in the unit.
- **topics** – These are shown across two pages and tell you the science you need to learn.
- a **'Test your knowledge' page** at the end of each unit – This has interesting questions to test what you have learnt.

At the end of the book there is a **glossary**. This has important science words for each unit and tells you what they mean. These words are shown in **bold** on the topic pages.

If I am not sure what a bold word means on a topic page I look it up in the glossary or ask my teacher.

How do I use the topic pages?

Each topic is shown across two pages and is set out in the same way.

The summary tells me the key things I need to learn and understand in the topic.

The words and pictures help me to learn more about science. I need to understand the scientific relationships that are described, and be able to link cause and effect. I need to be able to explain the ideas scientifically, using the correct words, diagrams and symbols, to tell others what I mean.

Bold words are science words that I need to learn and use in my own science work. I can look most of them up in the glossary if I am not sure what they mean.

KEEPING HEALTHY

Your heart and pulse rate

Every time your blood returns to your lungs it collects oxygen from them. The oxygen is needed by all your body to stay alive. It is your blood that carries the oxygen around to every part of your body. Your pulse rate tells you how fast your heart is beating.

What does your heart do?

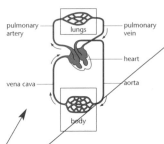

▲ This picture has been simplified to show the lungs as one box, and the rest of the body as another.

First of all your heart pumps your blood up to your lungs. The blood collects oxygen in your lungs, and then goes back to your heart.

Your heart then pumps the blood again. This time your heart sends the blood all around the rest of your body. The blood carries the oxygen with it.

Your body uses up much of the oxygen, so the blood must go back to the heart so it can be pumped through the lungs again to get more oxygen.

Exercise and pulse rate

Feeling your pulse Put your finger on a place where an artery is near your body's surface. You can feel the artery 'ticking' as your blood rushes through it. Each 'tick' you feel is one pump from your heart, so taking your pulse tells you how fast your heart is beating.

The number of 'ticks' you count in one minute is your **pulse rate**.

▲ One easy place to feel a pulse is in the wrist.

18

Many drawings have captions and labels. These help me to understand the pictures. I need to draw and label my own drawings like the ones in the book.

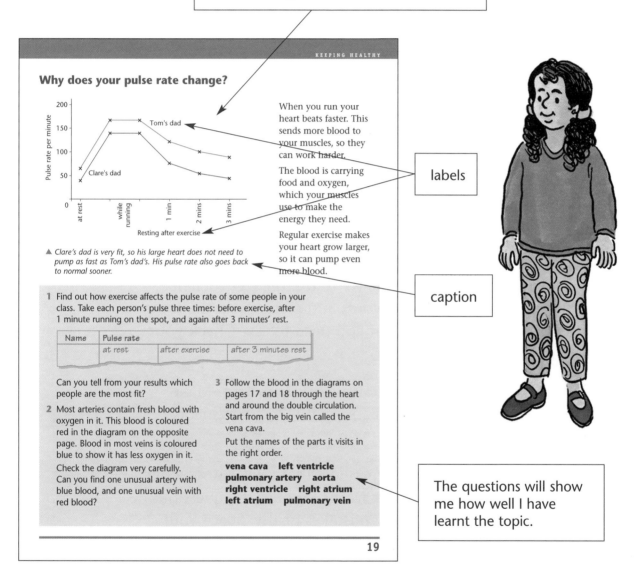

KEEPING HEALTHY

Why does your pulse rate change?

Pulse rate per minute

Tom's dad

Clare's dad

at rest | while running | 1 min | 2 mins | 3 mins

Resting after exercise

▲ Clare's dad is very fit, so his large heart does not need to pump as fast as Tom's dad's. His pulse rate also goes back to normal sooner.

When you run your heart beats faster. This sends more blood to your muscles, so they can work harder.

The blood is carrying food and oxygen, which your muscles use to make the energy they need.

Regular exercise makes your heart grow larger, so it can pump even more blood.

labels

caption

1 Find out how exercise affects the pulse rate of some people in your class. Take each person's pulse three times: before exercise, after 1 minute running on the spot, and again after 3 minutes' rest.

Name	Pulse rate		
	at rest	after exercise	after 3 minutes rest

Can you tell from your results which people are the most fit?

2 Most arteries contain fresh blood with oxygen in it. This blood is coloured red in the diagram on the opposite page. Blood in most veins is coloured blue to show it has less oxygen in it. Check the diagram very carefully. Can you find one unusual artery with blue blood, and one unusual vein with red blood?

3 Follow the blood in the diagrams on pages 17 and 18 through the heart and around the double circulation. Start from the big vein called the vena cava.

Put the names of the parts it visits in the right order.

**vena cava   left ventricle
pulmonary artery   aorta
right ventricle   right atrium
left atrium   pulmonary vein**

The questions will show me how well I have learnt the topic.

19

There are more questions on the 'Test your knowledge' page at the end of each unit. These will test how well you have understood the science you have learnt.

Things to remember

- **Read the words carefully.** You might not understand everything the first time you read it. Read each sentence slowly a few times. Then it should make more sense. If it doesn't, then ask your teacher what it means.

- It is important to make sure you **spell words the right way**. The words you must learn to spell are written in **bold** letters. Try to learn these words and use them in your own science work.

- Learn the **scientific facts** and try to understand the **scientific ideas** in each topic. Try to recognise **scientific relationships** in what you read and learn to **link cause and effect**. Try to use these ideas in your own science writing. You need to explain things clearly so that other people can understand what you mean.

- **Answer the questions well**. Always write in full sentences. Spell each word correctly. Always try to use the right science words in your answer. Use the words and pictures on the topic pages to help you work out what you need to say. Check your answer and try to make it better.

- **Use the correct ways of writing and drawing**. Make sure that you use the right units and symbols. Always label drawings clearly and properly.

- **Set your work out properly**. Follow the rules your teacher has told you for setting out your work. Number the questions in the right order. Cross out any mistakes neatly. Space your work sensibly on the page.

Keeping healthy

Before you start you should know that:

- animals are alike in some ways and different in some ways
- an adequate and varied diet is needed to keep healthy
- different animals have different diets
- the shape of teeth helps animals eat the foods they like
- bones help you stand up and move
- muscles make it possible for you to move
- changes take place in your body when you exercise

At the start of this unit you will learn about keeping healthy and:

- about the characteristics of living things
- about the organs in your body
- the importance of a varied diet
- about the circulation of the blood and measuring pulse rate

Later in the unit you will learn more about how humans move and:

- how exercise is important
- what muscles do when they work
- about the dangers of alcohol, smoking and drugs
- how micro-organisms can cause diseases

Characteristics of living things

Human beings are living things. What does it mean when we say that something is alive? All living things have to feed: animals eat food and plants make their own food. Living things also grow larger. They can move themselves, and also reproduce.

Why do animals feed?

Animals need to eat for many different reasons.

- Food gives us the **energy** we need to keep warm and to move around. It is our fuel, like petrol is the fuel in a car.
- Food gives us the material we need to grow. A house is made of bricks, but we are made of the food we eat. We need to eat to build our bodies.
- Food allows us to repair damage if we are injured. It gives us the material we need to grow new skin over a place where we are cut.

▲ *Clare needs plenty of food because she is growing. What is her dad using most of his energy for?*

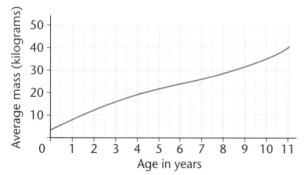

▲ *This shows the average mass of children at different ages.*

What is growth?

Mina had a mass of only 3 kilograms when she was born, but when she is an adult her mass will be about 50 kilograms. The extra mass will come from her food.

Plants grow too – a huge oak tree grows from a tiny acorn! Such a lot of growth takes a long time. Full-sized trees can be over 100 years old.

Movement

Living things move themselves. Animals use muscles to help them move. Plants can move parts of themselves too. Some flowers open in the day and close at night, and leaves move around to keep facing the Sun.

Clouds move across the sky but they are not alive. They are only being blown along by the wind. They cannot move on their own.

daytime   night-time

Reproduction

Reproduction means 'to make more'. Human beings reproduce by having babies. It takes nine months for the baby to grow inside the mother until it is big enough to be born. After that it needs to be looked after for many years until it can look after itself. Finally it will be able to have children of its own.

▲ Twenty-five years ago Jack's mum was pregnant.

▲ After Jack was born he fed on his mother's milk.

▲ While he was a boy his parents taught him how to do things for himself.

▲ Now Jack and his wife are parents.

1 Make a chart like this one in your book and fill it in.
Then add five more things of your own.

	Does it feed?	Does it move?	Does it grow?	Does it reproduce?	Is it alive?
Human					
Tree					
Wind					
Butterfly					
Moon					

Your body's organs

Your body has many different organs. Each one has its own special job to do. They all work together to keep you alive. Important organs are the brain, the heart, the lungs, the kidneys and a whole group of organs called the digestive system. Plants have organs too – a leaf is the organ that makes food for a plant.

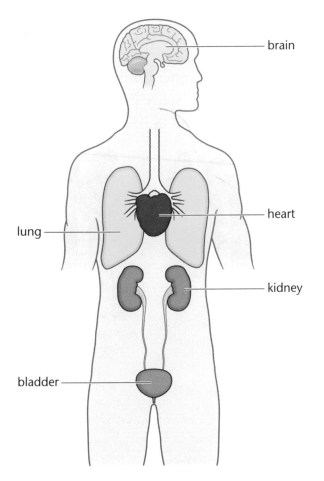

▲ *Some of your body's organs.*

What do we look like inside?

Your **brain** is the place where all your thoughts and feelings happen. The working parts are called **nerves**. Other nerves join your brain to the rest of your body. Nerves from your fingers bring messages to your brain so that you know what you are touching. If you want to move your fingers your brain also sends messages out to tell your muscles what to do.

Your **heart** is a pump. It pumps blood around your body.

Your lungs are for breathing. In your lungs oxygen from the air can move into your blood. Then your blood carries the oxygen to the rest of your body.

Your kidneys clean your blood. They take waste chemicals and some water out of the blood and pass them to your bladder. The bladder stores the liquid (called urine) until you are ready to go to the toilet.

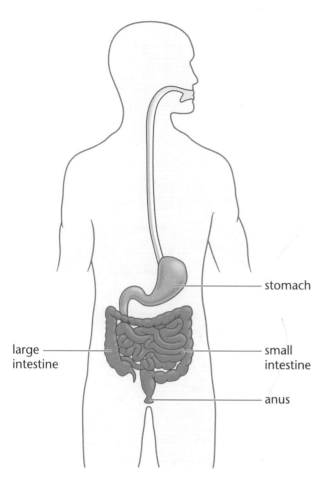

stomach

large intestine

small intestine

anus

▲ *The organs in your digestive system.*

What is the digestive system?

Many different **organs** make up the **digestive system**. Their job is to take the goodness out of your food so that it can go to the rest of your body.

These organs are part of a long tube called the gut (alimentary canal) which passes the food through your body.

Your teeth chew your food up so you can swallow it. The food then goes to your stomach where it is broken into smaller pieces by special chemicals. This is called digestion.

An adult's small intestine is about 8 metres long, and is curled round and round so that it all fits in! The small intestine finishes digesting your food so that it can pass into your blood. The blood takes the food to the rest of your body.

The large intestine absorbs water from what is left and passes it into your blood.

1 Copy this paragraph into your book and fill in the missing words using the correct words from these two pages.

The teeth, stomach and intestines are all .... that make up your .... system. Between them they share the job of digesting your .... and absorbing it into your .... Once it is in your blood the dissolved food can travel to any part of your body. The blood is moved around when it is pumped by your .... Waste chemicals build up in your blood; these can be removed by your .... They form a liquid called .... , which you store in your .... before going to the toilet.

Diets

A diet is what we eat and drink. We need to eat a varied diet which includes a range of different foods to keep our body healthy. Different types of food do different jobs. We must eat some of each. Too much food of one type, or a lack of a type of food, can cause diseases.

What caused scurvy?

In the 18th century it was normal for sailors to spend many months at sea. Their **diet** was poor as they mostly had to eat stored food and had no fresh fruit or vegetables.

Many sailors got a very unpleasant disease known as **scurvy**. They became weak, their gums became spongy and started to bleed, their teeth fell out and their joints became swollen. Sailors who had this disease usually died.

In 1753, a doctor decided to try to cure scurvy. Some sailors were given sea water, some cider, some vinegar and some lime juice. Those given lime juice did not get scurvy. Later it was found that limes, oranges and lemons, as well as other fresh fruit and vegetables, contained high amounts of vitamin C. This prevents scurvy.

What foods do we need?

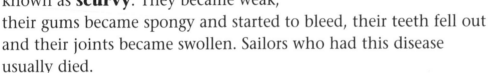

▼ For growth and repair　　▼ For energy for activity　　▼ To keep healthy

What makes a healthy diet?

Your **diet** is the food you eat and drink. Everyone needs a varied diet. Your body needs food to:

- grow
- repair
- get energy for activity
- keep healthy.

What happens if our diet is not varied?

Careful slimming is a good idea for overweight people. Most people only need to stick to a varied diet and simply not eat too much.

Fatty foods contain more energy than other foods. If you eat more food than you need for activity, the extra will be stored as fat.

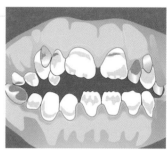

▲ Too many sugary foods like cakes, sweets, chocolate and sweet drinks can cause tooth decay.

Why do we need fruit and vegetables in our diet?

Fruit and vegetables contain **fibre**. This is needed to keep our intestines working properly. In Britain, people often do not have enough fibre in their diet. This can lead to serious complaints as they get older.

Fruit and vegetables also contain certain minerals and vitamins which are not found in other types of food. These are needed in small quantities in our food to prevent some diseases.

1 Use books or computers to find out why someone, in the 18th century, had the idea of giving sailors lime juice to cure scurvy. What tests did they use to find out how it could be prevented?

2 Look at the display of foods on page 14 and make a list of which types of food are needed:

- for growth and repair
- to give energy for activity
- to keep healthy.

3 Keep a diary of everything you eat and drink in one day. Would you say that your diet is varied? Is it healthy? Give your reasons.

Circulation of the blood

Your blood travels round and round your body in a never ending loop. Your heart pumps blood out to all parts of your body in tubes called arteries. It then goes back to your heart in other tubes called veins. Because your blood goes round in a circle, we talk about the *circulation of the blood*.

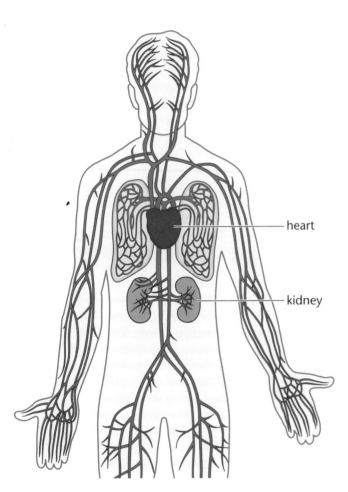

heart

kidney

▲ *Arteries carrying blood rich in oxygen are coloured red. Veins carrying blood with less oxygen are coloured blue.*

What does your blood do?

Your blood is your body's transport system. Many substances have to be moved around your body. For example the digested food from your intestines has to be taken to every other part of your body. It travels from one place to the other in your blood.

Where are your arteries and veins?

Arteries carry blood from your heart out to all parts of your body. **Veins** bring blood back to your heart again afterwards. In the diagram the arteries are coloured red and the veins are coloured blue.

Many veins are quite near to the surface, just under your skin. If you look on the back of your hand you might be able to see some.

Arteries are deeper inside. You can feel blood pumping through them when you feel your pulse. You learn how to do this on page 18.

How does your heart pump blood?

Your heart is a hollow structure mostly made of **muscle**. When it is pumping, it first relaxes to take in some blood from your veins. Then the muscle gives a squeeze and your blood is squirted out along arteries to other parts of your body. You can feel your own heart beating by putting a hand on your chest.

What does your heart look like?

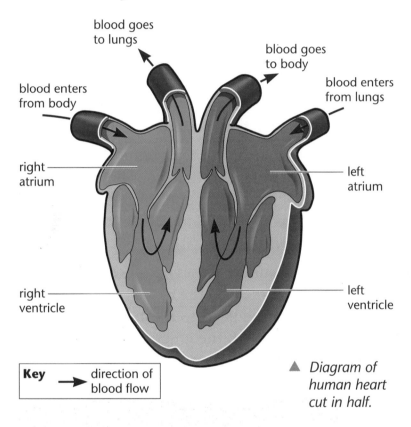

blood goes to lungs

blood goes to body

blood enters from body

blood enters from lungs

right atrium

left atrium

right ventricle

left ventricle

Key → direction of blood flow

▲ *Diagram of human heart cut in half.*

The heart is divided into four chambers called:

- the left atrium
- the right atrium
- the left ventricle
- the right ventricle.

In the diagram the *left* atrium is drawn on the *right* hand side. This is because of the way you are looking at it. Imagine that you are facing your friend. *His* left hand is on *your* right. You are looking at his heart in the same way as you look at the diagram.

1 What are the tubes called that carry blood away from the heart?

2 What are the tubes called that carry the blood back to the heart?

3 Why do we talk about the blood circulating?

4 Look in some books about the human body and see if you can find out the names of some of the blood vessels. Try these to start with:

- an artery taking blood to your leg
- a vein bringing blood out of your leg
- a vein in the neck bringing blood down from the brain.

See how many others you can find.

Your heart and pulse rate

Every time your blood returns to your lungs it collects oxygen from them. The oxygen is needed by all your body to stay alive. It is your blood that carries the oxygen around to every part of your body. Your pulse rate tells you how fast your heart is beating.

What does your heart do?

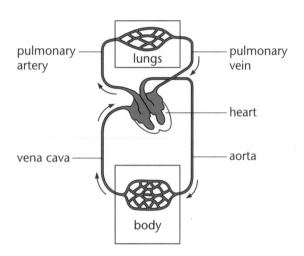

▲ This picture has been simplified to show the lungs as one box, and the rest of the body as another.

First of all your heart pumps your blood up to your lungs. The blood collects oxygen in your lungs, and then goes back to your heart.

Your heart then pumps the blood again. This time your heart sends the blood all around the rest of your body. The blood carries the oxygen with it.

Your body uses up much of the oxygen, so the blood must go back to the heart so it can be pumped through the lungs again to get more oxygen.

Exercise and pulse rate

Feeling your pulse Put your finger on a place where an artery is near your body's surface. You can feel the artery 'ticking' as your blood rushes through it. Each 'tick' you feel is one pump from your heart, so taking your pulse tells you how fast your heart is beating.

The number of 'ticks' you count in one minute is your **pulse rate**.

▲ One easy place to feel a pulse is in the wrist.

Why does your pulse rate change?

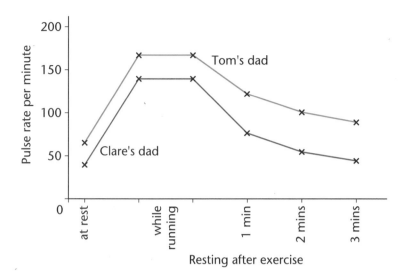

▲ *Clare's dad is very fit, so his large heart does not need to pump as fast as Tom's dad's. His pulse rate also goes back to normal sooner.*

When you run your heart beats faster. This sends more blood to your muscles, so they can work harder.

The blood is carrying food and oxygen, which your muscles use to make the energy they need.

Regular exercise makes your heart grow larger, so it can pump even more blood.

1 Find out how exercise affects the pulse rate of some people in your class. Take each person's pulse three times: before exercise, after 1 minute running on the spot, and again after 3 minutes' rest.

Name	Pulse rate		
	at rest	after exercise	after 3 minutes rest

Can you tell from your results which people are the most fit?

2 Most arteries contain fresh blood with oxygen in it. This blood is coloured red in the diagram on the opposite page. Blood in most veins is coloured blue to show it has less oxygen in it.

Check the diagram very carefully. Can you find one unusual artery with blue blood, and one unusual vein with red blood?

3 Follow the blood in the diagrams on pages 17 and 18 through the heart and around the double circulation. Start from the big vein called the vena cava.

Put the names of the parts it visits in the right order.

vena cava   left ventricle pulmonary artery   aorta right ventricle   right atrium left atrium   pulmonary vein

Exercise

Bones and muscles work together. Your muscles are joined onto the bones, and when your muscles pull on them you are able to move. When we exercise our muscles work harder. They need more blood flowing to them to bring oxygen and food, so your heart beats faster and your pulse rate is faster.

How do your muscles help you to move?

Your muscles always work in pairs. One muscle contracts while the second muscle relaxes.

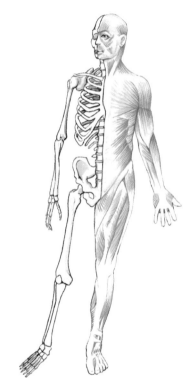

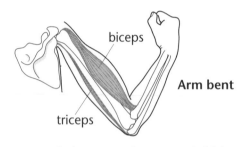

biceps

Arm bent

triceps

▲ Your biceps muscle becomes shorter and thicker. It feels harder. It is pulling and your arm is bent.
At the same time your triceps muscle relaxes.

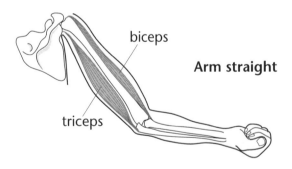

biceps

Arm straight

triceps

▲ Your skeleton is surrounded by muscles so you can move every part of your body.

▲ Your biceps muscle is soft and relaxed. Your arm is straight. At the same time your triceps muscle contracts.

What happens when muscles work harder?

When we exercise our muscles work harder. They need more blood to bring more oxygen and food to make energy. To get more blood to the muscles our heart beats faster.

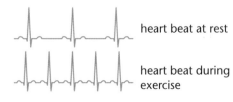

heart beat at rest

heart beat during exercise

How do we change during and after exercise?

If you run as fast as you can and then stop you will notice changes in your body. Athletes and sports men and women train very hard so that they will be able to work their muscles much harder for longer periods of time.

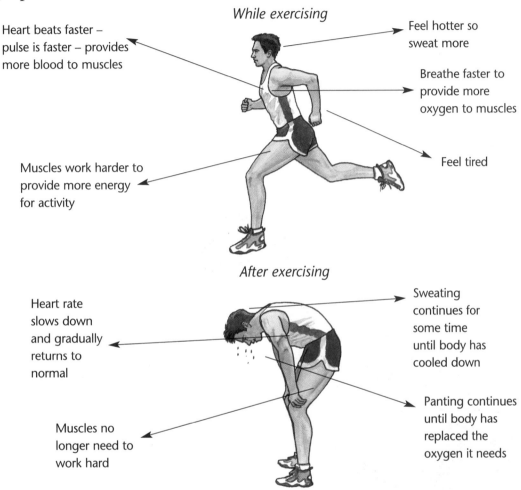

While exercising

Heart beats faster – pulse is faster – provides more blood to muscles

Feel hotter so sweat more

Breathe faster to provide more oxygen to muscles

Feel tired

Muscles work harder to provide more energy for activity

After exercising

Heart rate slows down and gradually returns to normal

Sweating continues for some time until body has cooled down

Panting continues until body has replaced the oxygen it needs

Muscles no longer need to work hard

1 Make a list of things you do every day which need your muscles to work.

2 Work out which bones move and which muscles you use when you
  - nod your head
  - swim
  - run.

3 Sara won the 100 m race at the school sports day. Describe what changes took place in her body while she was running and at the end of the race.

4 Find out what an athlete or a sports person does to train for his or her sport.

Keeping healthy

Everybody wants to stay healthy but sometimes people are tempted to do things that can make them very ill. For example drinking alcohol and smoking cigarettes can be very dangerous to your health. There are also some illegal drugs such as heroin and cocaine that are even more dangerous.

What is wrong with alcohol?

So many people drink alcohol that it is easy to forget how dangerous it can be. Alcohol is a drug that affects the brain. Drinking a little can make people feel warm, friendly and cheerful, but drinking a lot can cause problems.

▲ The policewoman is using a breathalyser to check the driver's breath for alcohol and make sure she is safe to drive.

How does alcohol affect the brain?

Even a small amount of alcohol slows down how quickly a person can react to something; it takes them longer to decide what to do. This is really dangerous if the drinker decides to drive a car. Many fatal road accidents are caused by drunk drivers.

What is an alcoholic?

An **alcoholic** is someone who becomes addicted to alcohol. This happens if they drink heavily almost every day. Their body becomes used to the alcohol, and soon they cannot do without it – they feel ill if they do not have a drink, and find it very hard to give up alcohol. In the end, the alcohol damages the person's liver and brain.

Why is tobacco harmful?

Smoking tobacco is another form of **drug addiction**.

People who smoke often find that it is hard to go for more than an hour or two without a cigarette. It is very difficult for them to stop.

Tobacco contains a drug called nicotine. It makes a person feel more relaxed, and it is the addictive part of the smoke. It can damage the heart. Smokers are three times more likely to die of a heart attack than a non-smoker.

Tobacco smoke also contains a lot of tar. This collects in the lungs and makes the smoker short of breath. It can also cause illnesses like bronchitis and lung cancer.

Every year thousands of people die from smoking.

▲ No thanks!

What other drugs are dangerous?

Doctors use many drugs properly to make people better. Some of those drugs are also abused, which means used wrongly. Two of these drugs are heroin and cocaine. They can both be used by doctors as painkillers for people who are seriously ill, but drug addicts take far too much and may die.

You should never take them!

1 Name four drugs that can cause addiction.

2 Write a letter to a smoker explaining why they should try to give up.

3 Some people think that they can risk smoking as long as they don't do it too much. Explain why they can end up smoking more and more so their health is harmed.

Disease

Some very small organisms can be harmful. These harmful micro-organisms cause many diseases such as tooth decay, measles and influenza. Diseases can be spread from one person to another in a variety of ways. Plants and other animals may also have diseases caused by micro-organisms.

What makes you ill?

There are many different illnesses but only some are caused by **micro-organisms**. The diseases caused by micro-organisms are those that spread from one person to another.

Viruses are so small that they are difficult to see, even with a powerful microscope. They cause diseases such as colds, measles, influenza, chicken pox and mumps.

Bacteria are small but can easily be seen with a microscope. They cause diseases like tuberculosis, whooping cough and boils on the skin.

Some **fungi** are moulds which cause diseases in plants. They are tiny threads which grow through tissues. In people they cause diseases like athlete's foot and ringworm.

Bacteria cause tooth decay

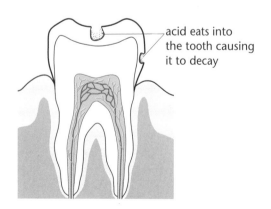

acid eats into the tooth causing it to decay

Bacteria feed on sugar on teeth and turn it into an acid. The acid eats into teeth and makes them decay.

Brushing your teeth in the morning and after meals removes the bacteria and sugar and so can prevent decay.

How do micro-organisms get into our bodies?

Micro-organisms get into the body mainly through the mouth and nose, or sometimes through cuts and wounds. Once inside they multiply very quickly and make the person feel ill.

▼ *These can all lead to the spread of germs.*

Why is it important to wash your hands?

Micro-organisms are known to be everywhere but only some are harmful.

There are some places where harmful germs are more likely to occur.

▼

Washing hands after touching things where germs occur is very important.

▼

A quick rinse under the tap is not good at getting rid of micro-organisms. A good wash using soap and water is important. Surgeons and people working with food are all aware of the need to wash their hands thoroughly.

1 Ask someone, like one of the school dinner ladies, how they avoid getting germs onto the food.

2 Choose one of the diseases mentioned here and find out more about it. What symptoms does a person with the disease have, and how can it be cured?

3 When someone has an operation they are more likely to catch a disease. All people in the operating theatre have to take special precautions. Find out more about what they have to do to avoid spreading germs.

Test your knowledge

1 Look through this chapter and find all the things to do with keeping fit and healthy. Make a list of all of them, and briefly say why each one is a good idea. Set your work out in a chart like this.

Healthy thing to do	Reason
Take exercise	Makes your heart grow stronger and larger.

2 This table shows the number of fillings in teeth for a class of 30 children.

number of fillings	number of children
0	10
1	6
2	5
3	5
4	3
5	1

Put the results into a bar chart.
What patterns do these results show?
What advice would you give the children with fillings?
How can they avoid getting more problems with tooth decay?

3 The picture on page 18 shows you how to find a pulse in your wrist. There are many other places in your body where you can find a pulse.

a Try to find some other pulses on your body.

b What must be near the surface, just under the skin, in places where you can find a pulse?

4 You might have seen robots in space films on the television. Sometimes they look quite real, and they can often talk to the other people in the film. It is not possible to build robots as good as that yet, but one day it may be.

Do you think a robot could ever be alive?

Use what you learnt in this chapter to explain your answer.

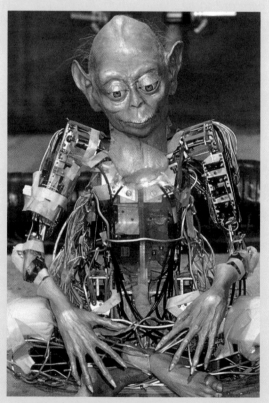

Living together

At the start of this unit you will learn about life cycles and:
- how plants make seeds
- how seeds are dispersed
- what happens when a seed germinates
- about the life cycles of a flowering plant and animals

Later in the unit you will learn more about habitats and:
- how plants make food
- how plants need different soil conditions
- what roots do
- how plants and animals are adapted to live in different habitats
- more about food chains
- more about using keys
- about micro-organisms and decay
- about micro-organisms and food

How plants make seeds

All plants must make more of their own kind for the species to survive. Many plants produce seeds which grow into new plants. Flowers with brightly coloured petals attract insects to pollinate the flower. The pollen is needed to fertilise the ovules so that seeds will form.

What is in a flower?

If you look closely at a simple flower you will find it has **sepals**, **petals**, **stamens** and **carpels**. Sepals protect the flower in bud and hold the flower together. Petals are often brightly coloured to attract insects like bees. The stamens make **pollen**.

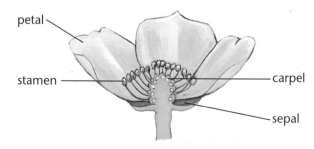

▲ *A buttercup flower cut in half.*

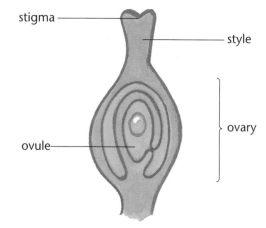

▲ *Diagram of a carpel cut through.*

In the centre you will find the carpels. Each carpel is made of a **stigma**, a **style** and one or more **ovaries**. The stigma is sticky to collect the pollen grains. The ovary contains an **ovule** which is like the egg of an animal.

To make a new plant, pollen from one flower has to fertilise the ovules in another.

How is a flower pollinated?

A flower must be pollinated before it can make seeds. Insects such as bees and butterflies carry pollen from the stamens of one flower to the stigma of another flower of the same type. This is called **pollination**. In some plants, such as grasses and many trees, wind carries the pollen between the flowers, not insects.

How do the ovules become seeds?

Each pollen grain makes a pollen tube. This grows down the style and into the ovule. Parts of the pollen and ovule fuse. This is called **fertilisation**.

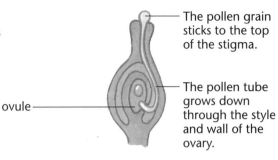

The pollen grain sticks to the top of the stigma.

The pollen tube grows down through the style and wall of the ovary.

ovule

The ovules then grow to form **seeds**. The ovary gets bigger and becomes a **fruit**. There are many different kinds of fruits. Some, like tomatoes, contain lots of seeds. Others, like pea pods, have only a few.

▲ *An ovule being fertilised.*

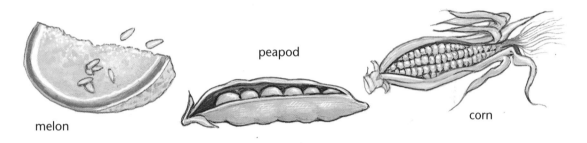

melon

peapod

corn

▲ *Fruits with their seeds.*

Seed dispersal

Seeds are dispersed by wind, animals or by the fruit bursting open to shed their seeds. When a seed finds the right conditions, it will start growing. This is called **germination**. It will grow to make a new plant of the same kind as its parents.

The sequence of a plant growing from seed, making flowers and then more seeds is known as its **life cycle**.

1 Why do some flowers have brightly coloured petals?

2 Describe how a bee helps to pollinate a flower.

3 What happens to the pollen when it lands on the stigma?

4 What do the ovules become after fertilisation?

5 Make a collection of as many different kinds of seeds as you can. Try to explain how each kind of seed is dispersed.

6 Make up a flow chart to show the life cycle of a flowering plant.

Seed dispersal

Seeds need space to grow into healthy plants. They have to be moved away or dispersed from the plant where they grew. The seeds can be dispersed by animals, wind or by pods bursting open. All plants make lots of seeds, but only a few seeds grow into healthy plants.

How are seeds dispersed?

By animals

All fruits have seeds inside.
Some birds eat brightly coloured fruits.
Some seeds are hard outside so they pass through the birds' guts and are dropped on the ground.

rose hip

elderberry

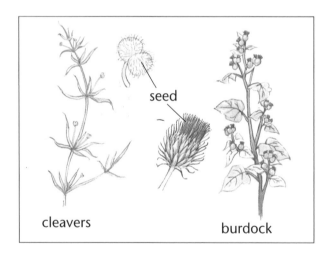

seed

cleavers

burdock

These seeds have little hooks that stick to animals' fur.

Many animals like to eat seeds.

Squirrels bury nuts in a food store. They often forget where the nuts are hidden and the nuts grow into new plants.

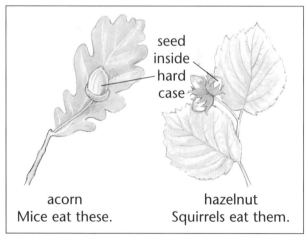

seed inside
hard case

acorn
Mice eat these.

hazelnut
Squirrels eat them.

By wind

These seeds are light so they can be blown away.

They are joined to a wing or a parachute which helps them to catch the wind.

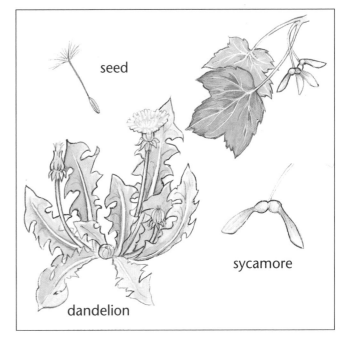

seed

sycamore

dandelion

By explosion

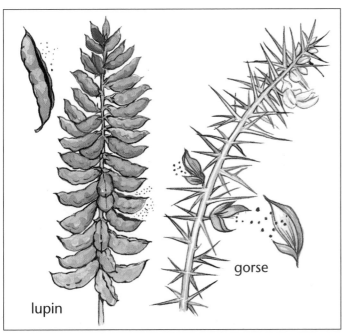

gorse

lupin

These seeds grow in a pod. When they are ripe the pod dries and bursts open or explodes. This flings the seeds away from the plant they grew on.

1 Explain why seeds need to be moved away from the plant they grew on.

2 How does the shape of dandelion seeds and burdock seeds help them to be moved away from the plant?

3 Why do the seeds inside rose hip fruits need to be hard outside?

Germination

When seeds are dispersed they may not germinate right away. This is when a young root and shoot first grow from the seed. Seeds germinate when conditions are right. In Britain this is usually in the spring when the weather is warmer. Seeds store food so that the new root and shoots can use the food store before the plant can make its own food.

What happens when a seed germinates?

The seed takes in water so that it swells. This makes the outer skin split.

A small root starts to grow, then a small shoot. This can happen while the seed is underground.

During this time the food store is used up.

Only when the seedling has its first green leaves in the light can it make its own food.

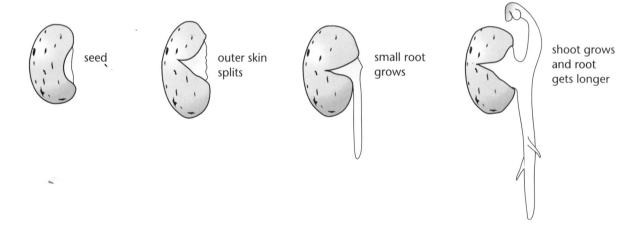

seed

outer skin splits

small root grows

shoot grows and root gets longer

Are all seeds the same?

You will know from looking at seeds you have collected that they do not all look the same. When they germinate they can look quite different from the bean seed shown above. Some seeds germinate very quickly, like cress which only takes a few days. Other seeds may not germinate for years.

What do seeds need to germinate?

Mina's class has been asked to carry out a fair test to find out what seeds need to make them germinate.

This is the investigation of Mina and Jack
They collected six flower pots and put the same amount of compost into each pot. They put one bean seed into each pot and then put them in different places. They watered some pots and left the others dry. After 10 days they collected their results.

Place	with water	germinated
by window	yes	yes
in refrigerator	yes	no
in dark cupboard	yes	yes
by window	no	no
in refrigerator	no	no
in dark cupboard	no	no

This is the investigation of Tom and Clare
Tom and Clare did their investigation in a different way. They filled three flower pots with compost and put the sunflower seed in each pot. They put the pots in different places. After 10 days they wrote down their results.

dark cupboard with water	seeds germinated
by window without water	seeds did not germinate
in 'fridge' without water	seeds did not germinate

1 Was Mina and Jack's investigation a fair test? Suggest how they could have improved it.

2 From Mina and Jack's results, what does it show that the seeds need to germinate?

3 Was Tom and Clare's investigation a fair test? What conclusions could they draw from their results? What advice would you give them if they did this investigation a second time?

4 Describe how **you** would carry out a fair test to find out what seeds need to germinate.

Life cycles

Both plants and animals produce young which grow to become adults. These adults can then produce young of their own. This is known as a life cycle. If living things did not produce young they would eventually die out and become extinct.

The life cycle of a flowering plant

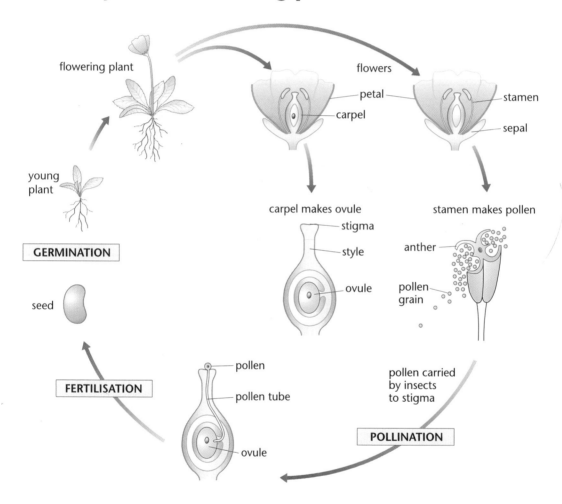

All flowering plants have a similar **life cycle**. Pollen is carried by wind or insects to a new flower of the same type. After pollination, the ovule is fertilised and then forms a seed. When the seed is dispersed, and conditions are right, the seed will germinate and grow into a new plant.

Life cycles of animals

Some animals need help from their parents for many years. The young depend on their parents for food and protection. Other animals like the butterfly lay their eggs and then leave them. The caterpillars have to look after themselves.

▼ *A human life cycle.*

Some animals that lay eggs look very different at different stages of their life cycle.

Some animals like these have babies that look very like the adults as soon as they are born.

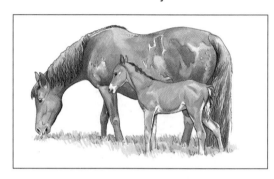

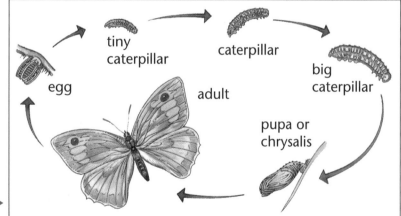

Life cycle of a butterfly. ▶

egg, tiny caterpillar, caterpillar, big caterpillar, pupa or chrysalis, adult

1 Try to grow a flowering plant that grows easily from seed, such as French marigold or nasturtium. Keep a diary of the changes that take place from germination, to flowering and producing seed. Draw pictures of each stage.

2 Collect photographs of yourself from when you were a baby up until now. Make a list of all the changes you can see.

3 Choose a different animal from the ones shown here. Find out as much as you can about its life cycle. In what ways is its life cycle different from yours?

4 Some animals like tigers and pandas may become extinct in the next few years. What does this mean? What can be done to stop this happening.

How plants make food

Sugars are the main food for a plant. The plant needs light to make this food. During daylight sugars are made in the leaves of plants by joining water from the soil with carbon dioxide from the air using the energy from the light. This process is called photosynthesis.

The importance of leaves

▲ *Leaves are arranged to trap as much light as possible.*

Most plants have green leaves. If you look up at a tree in the summer from underneath, you can see that the leaves form a pattern which fits together like a mosaic. In this way the leaves above cast as little shade as possible on the ones below.

This means that the leaves can collect as much light as possible. The light is the main source of energy for **photosynthesis**. It is collected in the leaf by the green colour (a pigment) called **chlorophyll**. Without chlorophyll a leaf cannot make sugars.

What happens in photosynthesis?

- Water from the soil travels inside the plant into the leaves.
- Carbon dioxide from the air passes through small holes into the leaves.
- The leaves must contain chlorophyll.

- Light either from the Sun or bright artificial light must fall on the leaves.

Sugars and oxygen are produced by photosynthesis. The oxygen passes out of the leaf through the small holes.

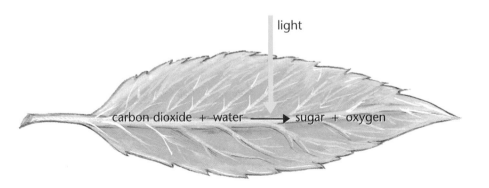

light

carbon dioxide + water ⟶ sugar + oxygen

What happens to the sugars?

Sugars are either changed to starch which can be stored in the plant, or used as building blocks to make all the other chemicals, like fats and proteins, that a plant needs to grow.

What happens if a plant has no light?

Jamal put a healthy lettuce plant in a dark cupboard for one week. He left another healthy lettuce plant on the windowsill. Each day he watered the two plants. After one week he put the two plants together and looked for any differences. This is what the two plants looked like after one week.

▼ *At start*

▼ *At start*　　lettuce placed in dark cupboard

▼ *After one week*

▼ *After one week*

From this Jamal concluded that plants cannot grow properly without light.

1 What is photosynthesis?

2 Write down what is needed by a plant so that it can make its own food.

3 Look at the drawings of the lettuce plants that Jamal used. Make your own record of the differences between the plant on the windowsill and the plant in the cupboard after one week.

4 Write your own conclusions about the experiment with the lettuce plants.

5 Clare's mum had two apple trees. Clare noticed that caterpillars were eating the leaves of one of the apple trees. The other tree they had left alone.

In the autumn, one tree had 50 large apples. The tree with leaves eaten by caterpillars had 20 small apples.

Try to explain why the damaged tree had fewer apples.

Roots and soil

Plants need different soil conditions for healthy growth. Plants need water and nutrients from the soil. These are taken up by their roots and pass up the stem and other parts of the plant. The roots anchor the plant in the soil to stop it being blown over.

What do plants need for healthy growth?

Different plants grow well in different kinds of soil. For example water iris needs damp waterlogged soil. Most other plants would die in these conditions as their roots would rot.

Heathers grow best on dry sandy soil but most plants would find these conditions poor as there would not be enough water.

WATER IRIS — Grow in rich damp soil in sun

SAXIFRAGE — Dry soil, well drained in sun

HEATHER — Dry sandy soil in full sun

BLUEBELL — Moist soil in shade or partial shade

RHODODENDRON — Acid soil, rich in humus, cool woodland conditions

ROSE — Clay soil with humus in sun

What is different about the soils?

Clay
fine particles, poor drainage, lack of air spaces, high in nutrients

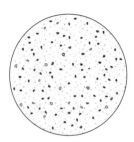

Sandy soil
larger particles, good drainage, larger air spaces, low in nutrients

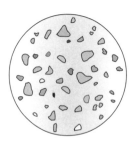

Loam
mixture of particles sizes, reasonable drainage, rich in humus (dead plants), high in nutrients

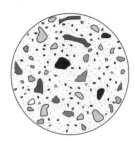

Roots need:
- air from air spaces in the soil
- water which surrounds soil particles
- **nutrients** which are dissolved in the soil water.

Why do roots need water and nutrients from soil?

Roots take in water from the soil. The water passes up the stem to the rest of the plant. In the leaves the water is used to make sugars which are the plant's food.

Nutrients are minerals dissolved in the soil water. The sugars made by the plant combine with the minerals to make all the different substances in the plant. So the plant can grow. Fertilisers can be added to the soil if it does not have enough nutrients in it.

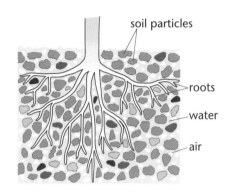

How do roots anchor the plant?

Damage like this was caused in October 1987 in Britain when we had some of the strongest winds we can remember. Many trees in the south of Britain were blown over, damaging houses, power lines and woodlands.

The roots of trees normally stop this happening. They spread out under the ground and hold the tree firmly in place.

1 Ten sunflower seedlings were grown in pots of soil. Five were given nutrients, the other five were not. The heights of the plants were measured every week for four weeks.

	1 week	2 weeks	3 weeks	4 weeks
with nutrients	6 cm	12 cm	22 cm	30 cm
without nutrients	5 cm	8 cm	14 cm	17 cm

a Why were five plants used in each condition?

b Plot line graphs to show the change in height for each condition.

c What conclusions can you draw from this experiment?

2 Look at the three soils on page 38. Which type of soil do you think would be the best for earthworms to live in? Give reasons for your answer.

3 Explain what would happen to a tree if it did not have a good root system.

Habitats

A habitat is a place where a group of living things are found. Examples of habitats are ponds, rivers, woodland, hedgerows and the seashore. The plants and animals found in each of these places are suited to their particular habitat. This is known as adaptation.

What lives in a pond?

A pond is one type of **habitat**. If you look closely at the water in a pond you will see many different animals and plants. The plants may be floating on the surface, or under the water, or growing round the edge. The animals may live in the pond or may visit it to find food and water, or to breed.

There are also many tiny plants and animals in the water. They are too small to see without using a microscope. We call them plankton and they can make the water look green.

The living things shown in the drawing are suited to the pond habitat. We call this **adaptation** – they are adapted to living in or by water.

▲ *This pond provides a home for many plants and animals.*

How are they adapted?

All the different plants and animals found in the pond will have special features to suit them to their habitat. For example:

- **fish** – this has a streamlined body, fins and a tail to help it swim through the water. It has gills for taking oxygen from the water. Its scales protect it from injury.

- **heron** – this bird has good eyesight and a long sharp beak so that it can catch fish. It needs wings so that it can fly to other ponds and streams in search of food.

- **water lily** – this plant has leaves which float on the surface of the pond so that it can get the light it needs for photosynthesis. Its roots grow in the mud to hold it in place.

What lives in a woodland?

The plants and animals in a wood are different from those you would find in a pond. There are trees and there are other plants which like to grow under the trees where it is shady.

There are many different places for animals to live in a wood. Some animals live on different parts of the trees, such as on the leaves, under the bark or in the flowers or fruits of the trees. Other animals live in the damp soil or on the plants under the trees. Birds build their nests in the trees and feed on seeds, fruits and insects. Animals such as deer visit the wood to feed on the leaves of the trees and other plants.

▲ *Many plants and animals are adapted to this habitat.*

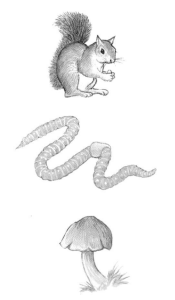

How are they adapted?

- **Squirrels** – these agile mammals are able to climb and leap between trees. Their teeth are strong, to crack open nuts for food.
- **Earthworms** – these animals have no legs and live in burrows in the soil. They eat dead leaves. They must stay damp so that they can take oxygen in through their skin.
- **Toadstools** – there are many different toadstools in woodland. They live on dead wood and leaves. They have long thin threads which break down dead matter and absorb nutrients. The part which we call the toadstool is for making spores which are like seeds in flowers.

1 What is meant by the word habitat?

2 What is meant by the word adaptation?

3 Describe how a fish is adapted to live in a pond.

4 Find out about another habitat, such as a rainforest or desert, and about some of the animals and plants that live there. Describe the conditions that they live in and how they are adapted to living in these conditions.

Food chains

Food chains show how one living thing is food for another. Nearly all food chains start with a green plant. This is the producer. The animals in the food chain are all consumers. In the chain each animal eats the one before it until the last animal which is the top carnivore.

Food chains in ponds

When we look in a pond we can find many different **food chains**. Here is one example.

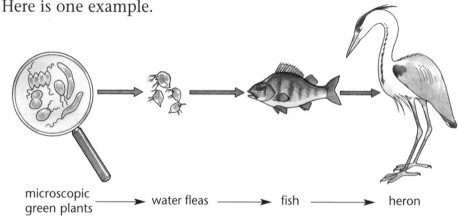

microscopic green plants   →   water fleas   →   fish   →   heron

The microscopic green plants make their own food so we call them **producers**. All green plants are producers. Animals are called **consumers** because they eat plants or other animals to get their food.

Herbivores are animals that eat plants and **carnivores** are animals that eat other animals. The animal at the end of the chain is called the top carnivore because nothing eats it. In this food chain the top carnivore is the heron.

If we take any carnivore we should be able to trace its food chain back to a green plant.

A lion is a top carnivore. Trace back through the lion's food chain until you reach a green plant. How many living things are there in the lion's food chain?

Remember the arrows in a food chain mean 'is eaten by'. The direction you draw the arrows is very important.

Food chains in a wood

This picture shows a woodland scene. Many different plants and animals will be found here.

Here is one food chain from this habitat.

leaves ⟶ snail ⟶ thrush ⟶ fox

What do they eat?

To find food chains in this habitat we need to know what each animal eats.

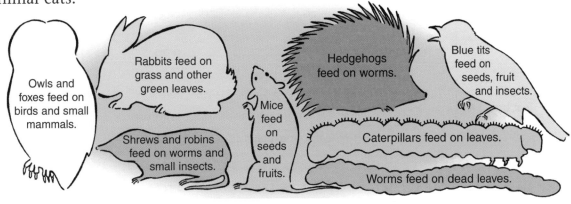

Owls and foxes feed on birds and small mammals.

Rabbits feed on grass and other green leaves.

Shrews and robins feed on worms and small insects.

Mice feed on seeds and fruits.

Hedgehogs feed on worms.

Blue tits feed on seeds, fruit and insects.

Caterpillars feed on leaves.

Worms feed on dead leaves.

A plant or animal usually belongs to several food chains. When you connect them together for any particular habitat you have a **food web**.

1 From the examples of food chains given on these two pages make lists of producers, herbivores and carnivores.

2 Why is the Sun important for all living things in a food chain?

3 Write down as many different food chains as you can in the woodland habitat. Remember you can use the same plant or animal more than once. Try to join some of your food chains together to make a food web.

Using keys

Keys are used to sort animals or plants into their correct group or to identify them. They can be branching keys or numbered keys. Branching (or spider) keys are useful when there is a small number of groups of living things to be identified. Numbered keys are better when there are more animals or plants to sort out.

Making a key

A **key** uses differences between the plants or animals you are trying to identify to split the group up into smaller groups. Other differences are used to split the smaller groups even more, until you are left with one plant or animal in the group. This one is then named.

Using a key

Here is a branching (or spider) key for the plants in the picture. Use the key to name the plants in the picture.

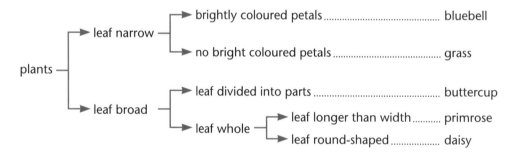

- plants
  - leaf narrow
    - brightly coloured petals .... bluebell
    - no bright coloured petals .... grass
  - leaf broad
    - leaf divided into parts .... buttercup
    - leaf whole
      - leaf longer than width .... primrose
      - leaf round-shaped .... daisy

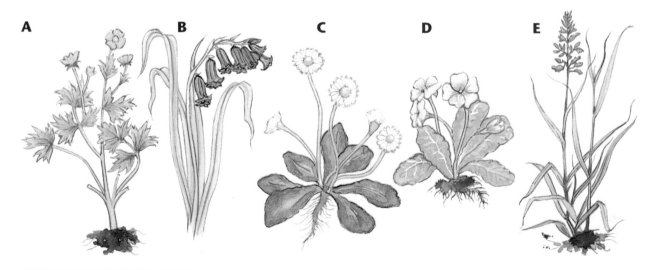

A   B   C   D   E

Using a key to identify children

Here is a numbered key for the children in the picture. It uses differences between the children to help you identify them. Use the key to name the children in the picture.

A

B

C

D

E

F

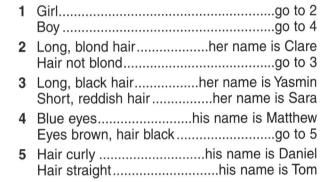

1	Girl..	go to 2
	Boy	go to 4
2	Long, blond hair...................	her name is Clare
	Hair not blond........................	go to 3
3	Long, black hair.................	her name is Yasmin
	Short, reddish hair	her name is Sara
4	Blue eyes........................	his name is Matthew
	Eyes brown, hair black..........	go to 5
5	Hair curly	his name is Daniel
	Hair straight.........................	his name is Tom

As long as the animal or plant you are trying to name is in the key, you should be able to identify it. A key will not be useful if it does not include the animal or plant you want to name.

1 What does a key do?

2 Use this key to identify these sea animals:

1	Animal with a shell..........................	go to 2
	Animal without a shell.....................	go to 3
2	Animal with one shell.....................	periwinkle
	Animal with two shells	mussel
3	Animal with tentacles......................	go to 4
	Animals without tentacles	ragworm
4	Animal with round body	sea anemone
	Animal with long body....................	squid

A

B

C

3 Look at the key to identify a group of children.
Produce your own key to identify a group of your friends.

Decay

As living things grow, much of the food that they make or eat is used for growth. They may be eaten by other animals or they may die. When they die their bodies are broken down by micro-organisms into simpler substances. This is known as decay.

What happens to dead plants and animals?

Some dead things are eaten. For instance, earthworms eat dead leaves and crows eat animals killed on roads. Micro-organisms feed on the rest of the dead things and break them down into nutrients and gases. The gases go into the air and the nutrients go back into the soil where they can be used by plants for their growth.

▼ Bacteria are so small that you need a powerful microscope to see them.

Bacteria and fungi are micro-organisms that grow on the dead bodies of plants and animals. They are very important. If they didn't break down dead things the Earth would be covered in them. There would also be no nutrients in the soil that plants need for growing well.

▼ Fungi

pin mould growing
on bread

mushrooms growing
on dead plants

What happens to an apple if it is left to rot?

This apple has just fallen from the tree.

Several days later it has turned brown and you can see bacteria and fungi on the surface.

After some weeks the apple has almost gone. It has been turned into soluble nutrients and gases.

What happens in a compost heap?

Compost heaps are built in gardens to remove all the dead plant material, like grass cuttings and waste vegetables. They are made into a heap to keep the inside warm and moist. They can be surrounded by wood or wire mesh, or be made inside a special compost bin.

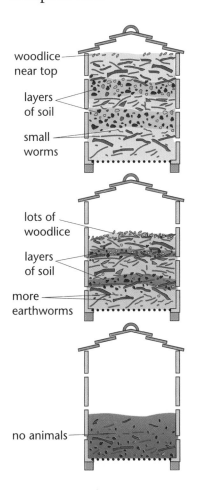

woodlice near top

layers of soil

small worms

lots of woodlice

layers of soil

more earthworms

no animals

A new heap is made with a mixture of dead plant material. Some soil is added at different levels to make sure that soil animals like worms and micro-organisms are added into the heap.

After several weeks, the volume of the heap has reduced. There are many small animals like woodlice and earthworms and millions of bacteria and fungi. The temperature inside the heap has got much higher because the living things give off heat.

After several weeks, most of the soil animals have gone but there are still many micro-organisms. The volume has reduced a little more but the heap is beginning to cool down. The compost will soon be ready to put on the soil to return the nutrients that plants need.

1 Explain what would happen if there were no micro-organisms in a woodland habitat.

2 What household waste can be put into a compost heap? Why is this better than putting waste into the dustbin?

3 Tom's parents put these things into their compost heap. Write down which of them would decay and which would stay unchanged after several months. **grass, branches, plastic bottles, metal cans, plastic bags, newspaper, tea leaves, broken glass, potato peelings**

Micro-organisms and food

All the food we eat has come in some way from plants and animals, so it will decay if it is kept where micro-organisms can live and grow. Food must be preserved if we want to keep it for some time. Some micro-organisms, like yeast, are useful in making food.

What happens when food goes mouldy?

Bacteria and fungi make spores which are microscopic. These spores are all around us, in the air, in water and on every surface. If food is left uncovered the spores will fall onto the food. If it is warm they will begin to grow into more bacteria or fungi. In a few hours the food will begin to **decay** though you may see no changes to the food for a few days.

As well as decaying the food, micro-organisms growing on food can produce poisons which make us very ill.

How can we stop food decaying?

- Keep food covered.
- Store fresh and cooked food in a cool place or refrigerator.
- Make sure your hands are washed before handling food.
- Clean everything thoroughly that may touch the food.

All these foods can be stored and will not decay for a long time.

Yeast is a useful micro-organism

To make bread we need a micro-organism called yeast. We know it is alive because it grows and reproduces. If we look at it under the microscope we can see that it is made of tiny cells with buds.

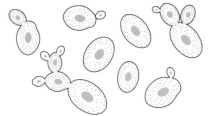

Yeast feeds on sugars. When it is put in a warm place with a sugar solution, the liquid will begin to bubble. This is because the yeast is releasing a gas called carbon dioxide.

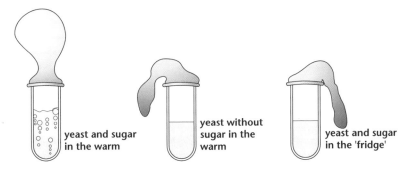

yeast and sugar in the warm

yeast without sugar in the warm

yeast and sugar in the 'fridge'

When we make bread we want it to be light. We use yeast and sugar added to the flour and water so that the bubbles of gas rise through the bread dough and make it swell.

Bread without yeast would be very heavy and not as nice to eat.

with yeast   without yeast

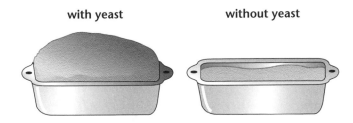

1 Complete these two sentences:

Micro-organisms are useful because

....

Micro-organisms are harmful because

....

2 Make a table to show ways that food can be kept without going bad. For each one explain your reason.
(Hint: think of all conditions that living things usually need to grow well.)
The first one has been done for you.

Method	Reason
dried food	no water for micro-organisms to grow

Test your knowledge

1 Make a crossword using all or some of these words.

**sepal   petal   carpel   stamen
ovary   ovule   seed**

Write clues for each word. You could start your crossword like this:

S	E	P	A	L
	E			
	T			
	A			
	L			

2 Farmer Joe needed some new land to grow wheat. He had some woodland on his farm which he cut down to make more room for his crops.

For each of the first five years the wheat grew well but the next year it didn't.

a   Why do you think the wheat stopped growing as well as it had for the first five years?

b   What could Farmer Joe do to the land to get a better crop of wheat?

c   Why did the trees grow well in the woodland before it was cut down? (Clue – look at the pages on decay.)

3 Design a poster to display in a doctor's waiting room giving advice on how to avoid micro-organisms getting onto food.

4 Write down a food chain from one habitat you have studied. (Make sure you draw the arrows in the right direction.)

a   For each of the living things you have named, write down whether it is a *producer* or a *consumer*.

b   Write down the name of a *herbivore* in your food chain.

c   Write down the name of the *top carnivore* in your food chain.

d   Explain how each of the living things in your food chain is adapted to the habitat where it lives.

5 Imagine you have travelled to another planet rather like Earth. On this planet you have found a habitat which is warm and damp with tall trees and ponds. Draw or describe five of the animals living there and explain how you think they are adapted to this habitat.

6 Look at these five shapes. Find out what each one is called. Construct your own key so that someone who does not know the names would be able to use it.

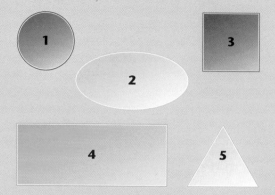

Gases and changing states

At the start of the unit you will learn more about gases and that:
- gases are different from solids and liquids
- materials can exist in more than one state
- soils have air trapped in them
- air is a gas and is all around us
- there are many useful gases as well as some that are harmful

Later in the unit you will learn more about how materials change their physical state and that:
- changes of state are brought about by heating or cooling a material
- melting, freezing, evaporating and condensing are changes of state which can be reversed
- evaporation happens when a liquid turns into a gas
- condensation happens when a gas changes into a liquid
- the water cycle tells the story of how water travels in different states from place to place

Solids, liquids and gases

All materials are either a solid, a liquid or a gas.
Solids keep their shape unless a force is applied to them.
Liquids pour and take the shape of the container they are in.
Gases spread out and fill all the space around them.

Solids

Solids are made of particles which are packed together very tightly.

Daniel had four balls of plasticine, all of the same shape, size and weight. As plasticine is a solid, he could change the shape of the balls only by applying a force. He used pushes and pulls. Although he changed the shape, the amount of plasticine was still the same.

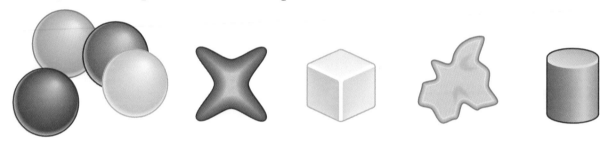

Liquids

Liquids are made of particles that are not packed as tightly as those in a solid. So a liquid can pour and take up a different shape. Mina had 100 ml of water. She poured it into a tall, thin container. The water took the shape of the container. Then she poured it into other containers. Each time the water took the shape of the container.

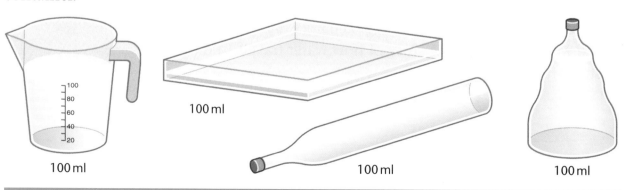

100 ml

100 ml

100 ml

100 ml

Gases

Gases cannot usually be seen. To prove they are there Daniel put an empty bottle into a bowl of water. He noticed that bubbles were coming out of the bottle. These were air bubbles. The bottle was not empty, it was full of air.

Gases have particles which are loosely joined together. They spread out to fill all the space available.

Mina sprayed some perfume into the corner of a room. She asked Daniel to stand in another corner and tell her when he could smell the perfume. Mina could smell it straight away. As the perfume slowly spread across the room Daniel could smell it too.

1 Name two solids, two liquids and two gases you use every day.

2 Explain in your own words why solids, liquids and gases behave differently.

3 Why couldn't Daniel smell the perfume at the same time as Mina? Use the idea that gases contain small particles to help explain your answer.

Useful states

All materials are found as solids, liquids or gases. These are called the physical states of matter. The particles in a solid are found in a set pattern and are close to each other. In a liquid they are further apart and can move more quickly. In a gas they are even further apart and spread out to fill the space they are in.

How are solids, liquids and gases different?

Jamal has been thinking about the differences between solids, liquids and gases, the three **states** of matter, since his teacher showed him what the particles might look like.

particles in a solid   particles in a liquid   particles in a gas

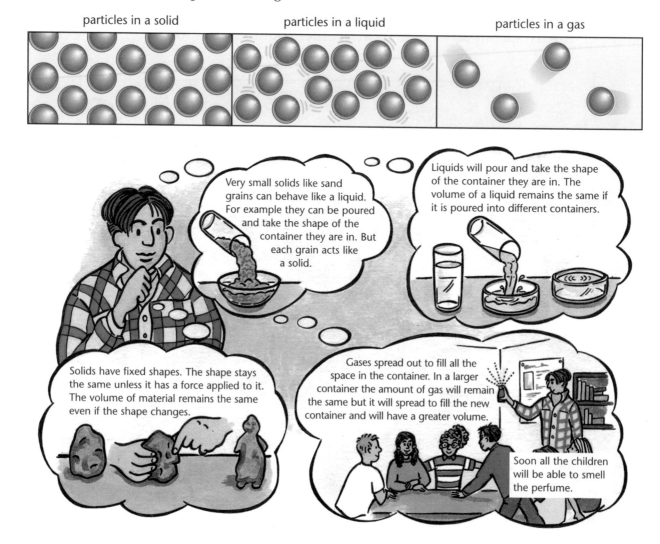

Very small solids like sand grains can behave like a liquid. For example they can be poured and take the shape of the container they are in. But each grain acts like a solid.

Liquids will pour and take the shape of the container they are in. The volume of a liquid remains the same if it is poured into different containers.

Solids have fixed shapes. The shape stays the same unless it has a force applied to it. The volume of material remains the same even if the shape changes.

Gases spread out to fill all the space in the container. In a larger container the amount of gas will remain the same but it will spread to fill the new container and will have a greater volume.

Soon all the children will be able to smell the perfume.

How is this knowledge useful?

Jamal then thought about solids, liquids and gases in a car and why they were there. He remembered the science he had learnt in school.

The liquid (petrol) in the tank takes on the shape of the tank. This makes it easier to store the petrol. The petrol can also travel through pipes to the engine. Solids would not do this.

The solid (glass) in the windscreen has a fixed shape which does not change unless a force is applied to it. This is useful because it keeps the wind out of the car. A liquid would not be able to do this. It would try to take the shape of the container and would flow into the car. (What a silly thought!)

The gas (air) in the tyres makes a smoother ride when the car goes over bumps because the gas can be squashed. Solids or liquids would not do this as they can't be squashed.

1 Explain the main differences between:
- a solid and a liquid
- a liquid and a gas
- a gas and a solid

2 Choose two solids which are used in a car. Now think of some reasons why it is important that they are solids.

Now do the same for two liquids and for two gases.

What's in the gaps?

Powders and sponges are examples of solids with air in the gaps inside the materials. These have big gaps so you can often see how easy it is for the gas to get inside. Soil also has big gaps and can take in air or a liquid such as water. Sometime the gaps are very small but air can still get in between the spaces.

Where are the gaps?

Look at these marbles. You can see the big spaces or **gaps** in between them. The spaces are not empty though. They are filled with the gases from the air, which move easily in and fill the spaces.

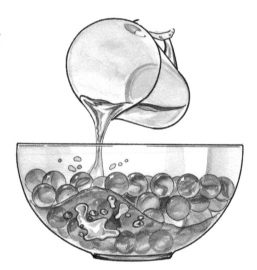

If you poured water onto the marbles the water would take the place of the air, pushing it out.

The volume of water you could pour in would be the same as the volume of air that has been pushed out.

Experimenting at home

Jack tried some experiments at home.

First he took a dry sponge and squeezed it out under water. He saw lots of bubbles come out and could see the gaps inside the sponge with his eyes. Water had taken the place of the air in the gaps.

Next he filled a balloon with air and left it for several days. When he came back he found that the air had escaped and the balloon had gone down. He couldn't see any gaps in the balloon. That made him think hard!

How much air is trapped in soil?

Air can get trapped in the spaces between particles of soil. Class 5 have been asked to think of a good way of finding out exactly how much air soil holds. Here is how Sara did the test.

I asked permission to get three soils from around the school. They were:

- sandy soil from near the sandpit
- clayey soil from the end of the school field and
- loamy soil from the flower beds.

I took some soil and poured water slowly into it until it drove out all the air. If I know the volume of water I poured in then this will be the same as the volume of air which has come out. I knew when all the air had been driven out because no more bubbles appeared and drops of water showed on the top.

To make the test fair I needed to:

- take the same volume of each soil
- make sure the soils were dried in the air for the same amount of time.

I thought I might make some mistakes the first time, so I repeated my tests again. After four tries the results were quite similar so I was pretty sure the measurements were good.

Here are my measurements.

Type of soil	Volume of water in the jug at the start (in cm³)	Volume of water in the jug at the end (in cm³)
Sandy soil from near the sand pit	500	100 110 100 105
Clayey soil from the school field	500	250 250 244 248
Loamy soil from the flower bed	500	175 180 190 185

1 How do you think Jack explained why the balloon went down after several days?

2 Use Sara's results to work out which soil had the most air gaps inside it.

3 How good were her measurements? Why did she repeat them several times?

4 How do you think she explained her results using the idea that soils have gaps of air between the particles?

Gases all around you

Materials can exist as gases. Liquids form gases when they are heated and evaporate. Everyday gases have a boiling point that is less than the normal daytime temperature. Many gases you find around you are helpful to us. But beware, some gases can be harmful or poisonous to you and to the environment.

A day in the country

Miss Taylor and Mr Smith have taken their class for a weekend in the countryside. Besides having some fun they plan to do some science. They are spotting gases. How many can you find in the picture? There are at least ten.

Nearly everything changes into a gas when it is heated strongly enough. Gases can be very useful to us. They can be used as fuels, to give a 'fizz' to a drink or to push materials out of an aerosol can. Air is a mixture of gases, mostly **nitrogen**, **oxygen** and **carbon dioxide**. When you breathe in air you use the oxygen to keep you alive. Plants take in carbon dioxide to make their food. Some gases are harmful. The gases that come out of a car exhaust damage the environment. Gases in cigarette smoke will seriously damage your heart and lungs.

1 Make a table like this one in your class book. Look carefully at every part of the countryside picture and find as many gases as you can. Use the information you see to complete the table.

Gas	Where is it found?	What is it used for?	Useful or harmful

2 Use a CDROM or books from your library to find even more gases to add to your table.

Changing states

Melting, freezing and evaporation are all examples of changes of state. If a solid material is heated enough it will melt and changes its state from a solid to a liquid. When it is cooled, it freezes and its state is changed from a liquid to a solid. Evaporation changes a liquid into a gas. These changes can be easily reversed.

What are changes of state?

Clare was thinking what might happen if a material is heated. A material like chocolate would turn from a solid into a liquid. This is called a change of state. If liquid chocolate was cooled it would turn into a solid. This is another change of state. Other changes of state are when a liquid turns into a gas or a gas turns into a liquid. There were some important words in Clare's mind.

Melting
When a solid becomes a liquid. Heat is added to make ice (a solid) change into water (a liquid).

Evaporation
When a liquid becomes a gas. Heat is added to change water (a liquid) into water vapour (a gas).

Freezing
When a liquid becomes a solid. Heat is removed to make water (a liquid) change into ice (a solid).

Condensation
When a gas becomes a liquid. Heat is removed to make water vapour (a gas) change to water (a liquid).

Oh these changes take place all the time!

How do you change the state of a material?

If you want to change the state of a material you either have to heat it up or take heat away by cooling it. Solids are turned into liquids by heating them. Once you have turned the material into a liquid you can reverse the change of state easily by cooling the liquid. It will then turn back into a solid. All changes of state can be reversed.

Different materials change state at different temperatures.

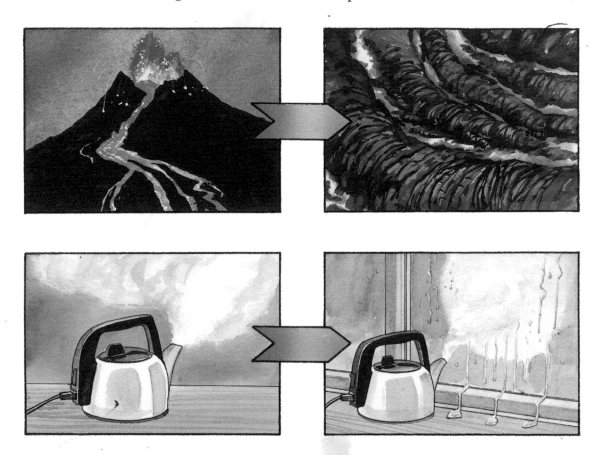

1 What change of state occurs when:
- wax runs down the side of a candle
- a puddle disappears
- you make ice cubes
- you boil a kettle of water?

2 Make a list of as many other changes of state you can think of.

3 Draw pictures which show water freezing, melting, evaporating and condensing.

Evaporating

Soluble substances like salt and sugar can be separated from liquids by the process of evaporation. As the water in the solution gets warm, tiny droplets of it turn into a gas called water vapour. The water vapour becomes part of the air leaving the salt or sugar behind.

Puddles

Tom saw that rain made puddles on his school playground. When the rain stopped, the puddles got smaller and dried up. Tom used chalk to draw round a puddle every hour to see what happened.

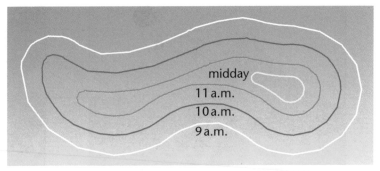

▲ Tom's puddle became smaller.

Tom's teacher said that the puddle dried up because the water evaporated. It turned into a gas and went into the air. The gas is called **water vapour**.

Evaporation causes washing to dry when it is hung out on the line on a sunny or windy day. On a hot day the water evaporates more quickly.

Evaporation can be speeded up.

On a hot day the higher temperature makes the water evaporate more quickly.	26 °C
A breeze blows the vapour away from the puddle so that more water vapour can move into the air.	

Can we get the sugar back?

Tom wondered if he could use evaporation to separate his sugar and water solution. He poured some of his sugar solution into a shallow dish. Tom put the dish next to the window where he knew it would be sunny and warm.

▲ *9:30 a.m.*   ▲ *3:30 p.m.*   ▲ *next morning*

Tom found that the water did evaporate. It dried up and left a layer of sugar in the dish. Tom carefully scraped the powdery sugar from the dish. The sugar was left behind because only the water could evaporate.

Tom tried the same test with some salt water. He weighed 5 g of salt and made a solution with water. He left it to evaporate and found that 5 g of salt was left after the water had gone.

Tom remembered that when he had paddled in the sea in his canvas shoes, the shoes had dried with a white mark on them. This was salt left on the shoes after the salty sea water had evaporated.

1 Write in your own words what happened to the water from Tom's puddle.

2 How can you speed up the process of evaporation? Draw and label pictures of two ways.

3 What is the best weather for washing to be hung outside to dry? Explain why in your own words using some well-chosen scientific vocabulary. Underline the science words.

Condensation and evaporation

Condensation and evaporation are reversible processes. Condensation happens when a gas cools down to form a liquid. The reverse process is called evaporation. This takes place when a liquid turns into a gas. We can see these two processes taking place all around us.

What is condensation?

Condensation happens whenever a gas cools and turns into a liquid. All gases will do this if you cool them enough. Scientists explain this by thinking about particles. The particles in a gas move quickly and fill a lot of space. When they are cooled they move more slowly, are much closer together and loosely hold on to each other.

You can see condensation happening when you take a bottle of milk out of the fridge. The water vapour in the air meets the *cold* surface of the bottle. The water vapour is cooled and forms droplets of liquid water on the glass.

How much water?

On a dry day there is only a little water vapour in the air. On a damp day there is much more water vapour in the air. Scientists explain this by thinking about particles. There are spaces between the air particles. The particles of water in water vapour can be in these spaces. There are more water particles in the spaces on a damp day.

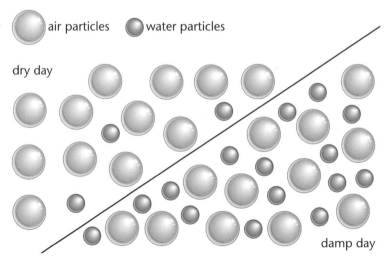

air particles   water particles

dry day

damp day

What is evaporation?

Whenever a liquid turns into a gas we say that it **evaporates**. Liquids, like water, evaporate faster on warm days. Scientists explain this by thinking about particles. As the liquid gets warmer the particles in the liquid get more energy. This means they can move about more. They may be able to move fast enough to break away from other particles in the liquid. If they are near the surface of the liquid, they will be able to escape into the air and become a gas.

It is possible to fill up all the spaces in the air with water particles. When this happens the air is said to be **saturated**. It is very difficult to get any more water to evaporate unless the air containing the water particles moves away. So it is easier to dry clothes on a windy day than on a still day.

---

1 Explain what it means if the air is saturated. Use diagrams if these will help your answer.

2 William's mother always says a windy day is best for drying clothes. Explain why she is right.

The water cycle

The water cycle is a continuous process in which water moves between the land and the air. The process has no starting or finishing point, it happens over and over again. This recycling of water means that rivers nearly always have water in them. So there is always water there to be cleaned for drinking.

How does the water cycle work?

(1) Heat energy from the Sun causes some of the water in lakes, rivers and the sea to evaporate. The water changes from a liquid to a gas.

go to 2

(2) The higher up in the atmosphere you go, the colder it gets. As the water vapour gets higher it cools and turns back into water. The water vapour is condensing. Droplets of water form and make clouds.

go to 3

(3) As more water vapour condenses, the drops of water get bigger. When the droplets get too big they fall to the ground as rain.

go to 4

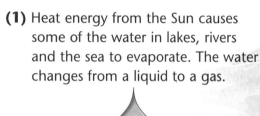

The **water cycle** works in this way because of the special properties of water. Water can evaporate and condense at temperatures which happen normally. Not many substances can do this.

Water is really wonderful stuff. We put it to many uses. If the water cycle ever stopped we would lose our supplies of drinking water.

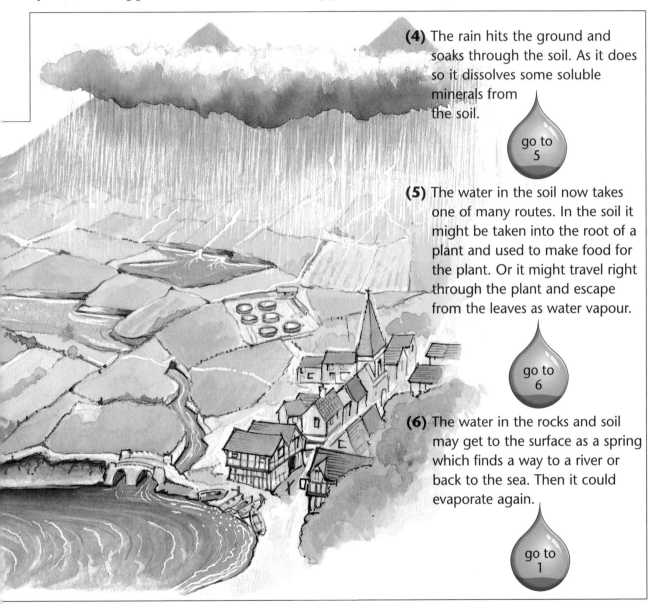

(4) The rain hits the ground and soaks through the soil. As it does so it dissolves some soluble minerals from the soil.

go to 5

(5) The water in the soil now takes one of many routes. In the soil it might be taken into the root of a plant and used to make food for the plant. Or it might travel right through the plant and escape from the leaves as water vapour.

go to 6

(6) The water in the rocks and soil may get to the surface as a spring which finds a way to a river or back to the sea. Then it could evaporate again.

go to 1

1 Explain how clouds form in the sky. Remember to use the words *evaporation* and *condensation* in your answer.

2 Write a short story about the journey of a particle of water round the water cycle.

Test your knowledge

1 There are many gases all around you. You may have heard the names of many of them.

Use books in your school library, CD-ROMs or the Internet to find out the names of some more gases and how they are useful.

Put the information you have collected together in an informative poster to display on your classroom wall.

2 Copy out the following cycle. Use the words below to help you label it correctly. Some words may be used more than once.

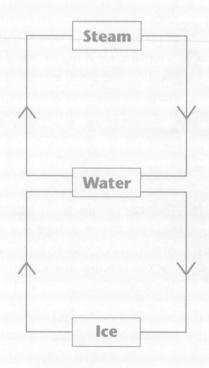

melts freezes 0 ℃ 100 ℃ boils

condenses heat put in heat taken out

3 Write sentences to explain the following:

(a) why bubbles come out of soil when you pour water into it

(b) the difference between a solid and a gas

(c) why you can soon smell perfume when it is sprayed at the other side of a room

(d) why water evaporates on a hot day quicker than it does on a cold day

(e) how sea water can eventually become clean water from the drinking tap in your house

(f) why milk bottles are covered in water when you pick them up from outside on a cold day

(g) why liquids take up the shape of any container they are poured in

(h) why air is a good material to put inside car tyres

(i) how clouds form in the sky

(j) what a saturated solution means.

4 You have just received a postcard from your friend Zoycletes of the planet Arcturan near Alpha Centuril. She plans to visit you soon. Her mother is worried about her washing her clothes whilst she is visiting you. She does not know the best conditions for getting the washing dry on Earth. They have no weather on their planet. Write an e-mail to send to her mother to explain scientifically the best conditions for drying washing.

Changes in materials

Before you start you should know that:

- some solids dissolve in water but others do not
- filtering is a good way of separating an undissolved solid from liquids
- dissolving, melting, evaporating and condensing are all changes of state
- some changes can be reversed, others cannot

In this unit you will learn more about scientific changes and that:

- dissolving is a change which can be reversed
- water can have many different materials dissolved in it
- when solids dissolve a clear (or sometimes a coloured) liquid is formed
- impure water can be made cleaner by using a sieve, a filter or evaporating the water to leave the impurities behind
- a water treatment works provides clean water to your home
- a solution contains a solvent and a dissolved material which is called a solute
- dissolving can be speeded up by stirring, by using smaller pieces of the solute or by heating up the mixture
- when a solid is dissolved in a liquid eventually no more will dissolve
- some changes cannot be reversed and these are called chemical changes
- burning most materials causes them to change into completely new materials, and the change is not reversible
- mixing some materials with water also produces changes which cannot be reversed
- irreversible changes often makes new and useful materials

Dirty water

Pure water is hard to find in real life. It usually has other materials mixed or dissolved in it. Puddles contain soil and dissolved materials. Ink has a dye dissolved in it and sea water contains dissolved salt. Dirty water can be changed into cleaner water by removing the impurities by using a sieve, a filter or by evaporation.

How can water be purified?

Class 6 have collected samples of water from different places. Only one is pure. They are thinking of different ways to make the water purer and how to get rid of the **impurities**.

I have got some distilled water. It is the purest water you will find. I have tried several ways of making it purer but I cannot make it any purer than it is!

You can see straight away that this dirty water is not pure. It was easy to remove the small stones and tiny soil particles from this water from a puddle. But I wonder if the water has anything dissolved in it?

distilled water

sea water

puddle water

pond water

Water is a very common liquid. It is rarely used in its pure state. We need to drink water to stay healthy. We also use water for washing ourselves and our clothes and other things. Water is very useful because it can **dissolve** many different substances.

1. What is another name for pure water? How did Jack try to make it purer?

2. How did Yasmin get the stones and small particles out of the water from the puddle? How could she find out if the water had any dissolved materials in it?

3. Why do you think Daniel thought sea water contained dissolved salt? How did he make sure his way of getting pure water did him no harm?

4. Michelle has worked out a good way of getting pure water from ink. Write out how she did this in the way you would normally write up an investigation. Make sure you use the correct scientific words to describe each step of the process.

5. Write sentences which explain what each word on the classroom board means. Use a scientific example if this will help bring out their meanings.

Clean water

We need clean water to drink and for cooking. Water is a mixture that contains soluble and insoluble substances. The insoluble substances can be taken out by filtering using a sand and gravel filter. These work in the same way as a sieve. Microbes in the water that might make you ill are killed by adding a gas called chlorine.

How is water made clean for drinking?

Michelle has drawn a flow chart in her book to show how water is cleaned to make it safe to drink.

Most dirty water has insoluble particles of different sizes in it. It may also have microbes living in it which could make you ill.

First the water is filtered to take out the larger insoluble solids. This leaves the very small insoluble particles that are spread out in the water and make it look cloudy.

The very small insoluble solids are removed by adding chemicals. This makes the small solids 'clump together' so they can be removed by filtering again.

If the water is to be clean enough to drink then any microbes in it must be killed. This is done by bubbling chlorine gas through it. (The chlorine is not concentrated enough to harm you.)

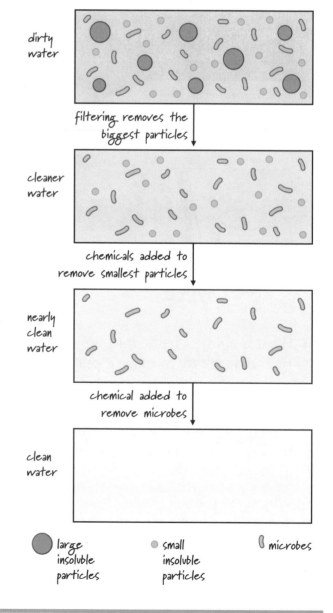

dirty water

filtering removes the biggest particles

cleaner water

chemicals added to remove smallest particles

nearly clean water

chemical added to remove microbes

clean water

large insoluble particles

small insoluble particles

microbes

The class trip to the Deer Dale water treatment works

Class 6 are interested in how dirty water is cleaned on a large scale.
Beverley from the Deer Dale water treatment works answers their questions.

What is the first thing you do?

We remove large pieces of dirt and other materials that are in the water. We filter the dirty water, just like you do in your classroom, only on a bigger scale. We have to change and clean the filters regularly so that they work well.

Do you do anything else?

We let the water settle in large ponds. Sunlight also helps to kill microbes. Some water treatment works add fluorine to the pure water as it helps to keep your teeth healthy. But we don't do this as as most people get this protection by brushing their teeth with fluoride toothpaste.

What do you add to the water and why?

Why does water from different places not taste the same?

First we add a chemical called aluminium sulphate. This clumps the very small particles of dirt together so that they can be removed by filtering. Then we add a gas called chlorine. This is poisonous but kills all of the microbes in the water.

Very pure water has no taste. If it has any dissolved solids or gases, it does have a taste. Water in different areas has different things dissolved in it, which gives it a flavour. Water from springs is often bottled because it is has dissolved substances which are good for you. The label on this bottle shows what is dissolved.

This tastes different!

1 Deer Dale water treatment works needs a leaflet to explain how water is cleaned so that it is safe to drink. Design a leaflet for them to explain what they do.

2 Explain how a filter that is made of gravel and sand can make water cleaner.

Solutions

A solution is made when a substance is dissolved in a liquid. Not all solids dissolve but those that do are called soluble. Solids that do not dissolve are called insoluble. The liquid part of the solution is called the solvent. A soluble solid which is dissolved in a solution is called a solute.

What does a solution contain?

All **solutions** are made up of two parts. They contain:
- a liquid which is called the **solvent**;
- a dissolved substance which is called the **solute**.

liquid particle   solid particle

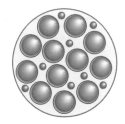

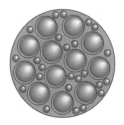

The liquid part (the solvent) is made up of very small particles. These are close to each other and always moving. They have small spaces between them.

The substance you want to dissolve (the solute) also contains very small particles. When you put it into the liquid the solute particles separate and spread out into the spaces between the particles of liquid.

When you add a solute to a liquid, at the start it all dissolves. This is because there are plenty of gaps in the liquid. As you add more solute the gaps fill up. After a while all the spaces between the liquid particles will be full and no more solute will dissolve. This is now called a **saturated** solution.

How much solute will dissolve?

This will depend on how much solvent you use. If you use more solvent there will be more spaces for the solute to move into. So you will be able to dissolve more solute.

Some solids are also more **soluble** than others.

How can you get more solute to dissolve?

If you can find a way of making the spaces between the solvent particles larger then more solid particles can move into them.

This can be done by warming the solvent. As the solvent becomes warmer the particles in the liquid move faster. This makes more space between them. So more solid can dissolve.

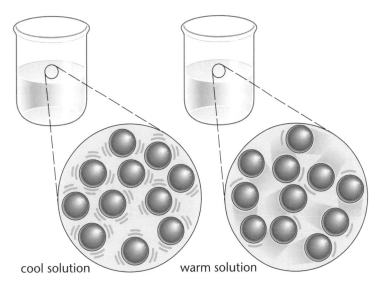

cool solution   warm solution

How can you make a solute dissolve quicker?

If you just put a soluble solid into a solvent it will take a long time to dissolve. If you **stir** the solvent the solute will dissolve more quickly. This is because stirring mixes up the particles of liquid and soluble solid so they are more evenly spread out. Stirring does *not* increase the amount of solute that dissolves.

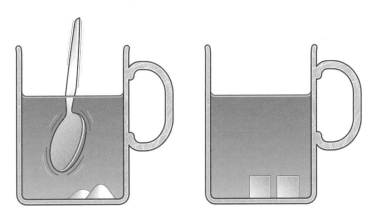

1 Neatly copy and complete this passage in your book. You will find the words you need below. BEWARE: you will not use all of them.

Some .... will dissolve. Solids that .... are called ....
Those that do not are called ....
The liquid part of a .... is called the .... A soluble solid that has dissolved in a solvent is called a .... Dissolving is when small .... of solid become spread out .... the particles of ....
When no more can dissolve the solution is called ....

**solids   saturated   dissolve
liquid   gas   between   soluble
particles   solute   insoluble
solvent   solway   solution
sulphur   solpress**

Speeding up dissolving

Some solids, like cooking salt, dissolve in water. You can dissolve about 35 g of salt in 100 cm³ of water. About the same amount of salt will dissolve in water at different temperatures. Stirring helps to speed up the dissolving as does breaking the salt into smaller pieces.

What's the problem?

Mr Smith has asked his class to think of tests to find out what makes salt dissolve faster in water. He has given them the following questions to help plan their thinking and writing.

I will investigate ……………..………

My prediction is ……………..

I made my test fair by ………….

My results show that ………..

Tom's test

Tom is not very good at doing scientific investigations. He sometimes gets mixed up, makes mistakes and misses important things out. Can you help him do better?

I will investigate dissolving by looking to see if stirring salt in water will make it dissolve quicker. I needed some cooking salt, fresh tap water, four beakers and a stop clock.

I took four beakers and put 50 cm³ of water and 10 g of salt into each one. I started the clock and stirred the first one 20 times. I then moved onto the second beaker and stirred the mixture 30 times. Then the third solution was stirred 40 times and finally the fifth beaker was stirred 50 times.

I made my test fair by taking the same amount of water each time I do the test and the same amount of salt 10 g. It doesn't matter how hot the water is.

I looked to see how long it then took for the salt in each beaker to dissolve. I put my results neatly in a table.

My results show that if you stir the salt it makes it dissolve more quickly.

Michelle's test

Michelle can write up a much better investigation than Tom. Here is how far she has got with her work.

I have seen people use sugar lumps or sugar granules to make their tea taste sweeter. The sugar lumps always take longer to dissolve. My idea is that dissolving happens quicker if you use smaller pieces of a material.

I will investigate how salt dissolves to see if large pieces of salt dissolve slower than smaller pieces. I have two different kinds of salt. Rock salt has large crystals and table salt has smaller crystals. I will break the crystals of rock salt and try to get enough which are half their usual size. My prediction is that the smallest pieces of salt will dissolve 10 times faster than the large rock salt crystals.

I put 50 cm³ of water at room temperature into a beaker. I quickly poured 10 g of rock salt crystals into the water and started the clock. I stirred the mixture until all of the salt had dissolved and recorded the time. It was hard to tell when all the salt had dissolved.

I did exactly the same with the other two kinds of salt and put my results in a table. Because I wasn't sure when all of the salt had dissolved I repeated the test several times. The table shows all my results.

Type of salt	Time salt took to dissolve in seconds		
rock salt	195	215	190
ground rock salt	95	110	95
table salt	45	39	36

1 a What did Tom miss out?

  b What was wrong with the way he timed the dissolving?

  c Should he have had a beaker with some salt and water which was not stirred?

  d Can you write a better prediction for him?

  e Can you explain his results better?

2 Write a paragraph starting with 'Michelle made her test fair by . . .'.

3 Using Michelle's table work out an average for each test she did.

4 Michelle had to make sense of her results by using a sentence which starts: 'My results show that ...' What do you think she wrote?

Reversible and irreversible changes

If you look carefully around you will see two kinds of changes. Sometimes you will see a material change in some way and then later it can be recovered in its original form. It has undergone a reversible change. Other materials change and cannot easily be restored. They have undergone an irreversible change.

Can you spot the changes?

There are lots of changes happening in this picture. How many can you spot? Think about the picture using the words that surround it.

BURNING   MELTING   BUBBLING   EVAPORATING   BREATHING

FREEZING   SOLIDIFYING   CONDENSING   GROWING   MIXING

Look for materials which are:
- being **mixed**
- **burning**
- changing state, and
- reacting.

How do materials change when they are mixed with other materials?

When sugar, salt or powder paint are added to water they change. They all dissolve in water to form a solution. You can get the original material back, quite easily, by evaporating off the water. The change is **reversible**.

When other materials are mixed together they become completely new materials. It is very hard to change them back into the original materials. The changes are **irreversible**.

All of these changes are irreversible.

How do materials change when they are heated?

Ice, chocolate and wax melt from solid to liquid when heated gently. When they cool the liquid returns to its solid state. These changes are easily reversed.

Other materials change much more when you heat them. Some, like paper, catch fire and burn so that they change forever. The change is irreversible.

Heating makes these materials change forever into something new.

1 Explain the difference between reversible and irreversible change.

2 Make a list of five reversible and five irreversible changes you can see in the picture on the left. Think of some more changes and add them to the right parts of your list. Try to make your lists as long as you can.

Chemical changes

A change in colour, a new smell, bubbles and substances getting hot by themselves are all signs that a chemical change is taking place. Burning is another chemical change which is irreversible. When gas is burnt with plenty of air the flame is blue. The gas is changed into water and carbon dioxide. When there is less air the gas burns with a yellow flame and makes smoke as well as some carbon dioxide and water.

How can you spot a chemical change taking place?

When a chemical change happens you might:

- see the colour of the substances change
- see a gas being given off
- see the substances burning
- see heat being produced
- see a new substance being made.

Tom is looking at a chemical change. He can see the bubbles of gas and can hear fizzing. Marble chips and lemon juice react together to make a gas. The gas made in this reaction is called carbon dioxide.

What happens when cooker gas burns?

Cooker gas is made from substances called carbon and hydrogen. In this gas they are joined together in a simple way. Cooker gas is easy to light and burns with a blue flame. All of it changes into new materials when it burns. While it is burning the gas joins with oxygen from the air to make the new substances which are carbon dioxide and water.

What happens when you burn wax?

Wax also contains carbon and hydrogen. In wax they are joined together in a more complicated way. Wax is quite easy to light and burns with a yellow flame. When wax burns not all of it is changed into carbon dioxide and water. Some carbon is not burnt and makes smoke.

What happens when you burn wood?

Wood is another material which contains mostly carbon and hydrogen. In this case they are joined together in a very complicated way. Wood is quite hard to light and some parts of it do not burn well at all. These parts are called ash and are left over when wood is burnt. Some carbon is not burnt and makes smoke.

1 Write down a list of things you might see happening when a chemical change happens.

2 Describe what happens when you burn cooker gas, wood or wax.

Draw a table to show changes that are the same and changes that are different when you burn these substances.

Test your knowledge

1 Make a table like this one. Look through this chapter and the last one on gases and changing states. Find as many changes as you can and fill in the table, making it as big as you can.

Change you see	Reversible or irreversible	What can you say about the change?
Ice melting	Reversible	This involves solid water changing into a liquid. To do this the ice needs heat to be given to it. It is a physical change.
Wood burning	Irreversible	When you burn wood brand new materials are made. You can never get the wood back. It is a chemical change.

2 Tom has some blue crystals in his chemistry set that he was given for his birthday. He did an experiment. He wanted to know how much of the blue crystals would dissolve in water at 20°C and how much would dissolve at 50°C. Here are his results.

Temperature in °C	Amount dissolved in grams
20°C	6 g
50°C	12 g

Tom stirred both experiments for the same amount of time. Try to explain his results. Remember to say why he stirred both experiments.

3 What would you look for in each of these changes that would convince you it was a chemical change?

boiling an egg
cooking a cake
burning a candle
mixing Andrews liver salts to water
iron rusting

4 Make a flick book to show a substance dissolving in water. Cut out 25 pieces of paper all of the same size and staple them together at one end. On each page draw a beaker of water, making sure to draw each one the same. On page 1 draw some salt in the beaker. As you gradually go through the book show more and more of the salt dissolving.

Try out your flick book to see if it works.

If you have time you could make another flick book showing the mixture being stirred or blue crystals gradually dissolving to make a blue solution.

Our Earth and the solar system

Before you start you should know that:

- the Sun is a star, much bigger than the Earth and far away
- the Moon is smaller than the Earth and closer to us than the Sun
- every day the Sun rises in the east and sets in the west
- the Earth orbits the Sun and the Moon orbits the Earth
- the Sun lights up our side of the Earth during daytime
- shadows are formed when the light from the Sun is shaded by an object
- there are four seasons called spring, summer, autumn and winter

In this unit you will learn:

- what is meant by the solar system
- about the complex structure of the Sun
- that the Earth is one of nine planets which orbit the Sun
- more about the orbits of the planets around the Sun
- the difference in structure between the inner and outer planets
- that the Moon takes about 28 days to orbit the Earth
- how the phases of the Moon are caused
- how the same face of the Moon always points towards the Earth
- how lunar and solar eclipses happen
- why a day is 24 hours long
- why daylight is shorter at some times in the year
- that the Earth spins around its own axis and that this causes night and day
- what causes the four seasons of the year
- what is meant by an equinox and a solstice.

The solar system

Our Earth is one of nine planets that orbit the Sun. This group of a star and planets is called our solar system. Deep in outer space there are other solar systems. Planets move around the Sun in almost circular paths called orbits. The further a planet is from the Sun the longer it takes to complete an orbit.

What do we know about our Sun?

At the centre of our **solar system** is a **star** which we call the Sun. The Sun is 150 million kilometres away from us. It is massive and has a diameter of 1 393 000 kilometres. Our Sun was probably formed from a large cloud of gas about 5000 million years ago.

Never look at the Sun directly with your eyes. It is very dangerous. The very bright light **could make you blind**.

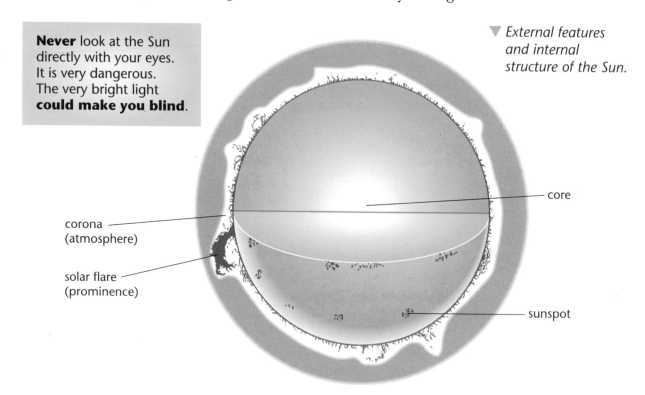

▼ External features and internal structure of the Sun.

corona (atmosphere)

solar flare (prominence)

core

sunspot

The Sun has a complex structure. On the outside there is a thin atmosphere of the gases hydrogen and helium. On the surface there are sunspots and solar flares (prominences). Deep inside, very high temperatures are generated by a non-stop nuclear reaction which releases huge amounts of energy. You see some of this energy as light and feel some of it as warmth.

What do we know about the orbits of the planets?

The Earth is one of nine **planets** that **orbit** the Sun. The other planets in our solar system are Mercury, Venus, Mars, Jupiter, Saturn, Uranus, Neptune and Pluto. Planets produce no heat or light of their own but they do reflect the sunlight which strikes them. The force of gravity between the Sun and the planets keeps them in orbit around the Sun.

The orbits of the planets (except Pluto):

- are almost (but not exactly) circular;
- lie on about the same level;
- do not cross over each other;
- are very predictable.

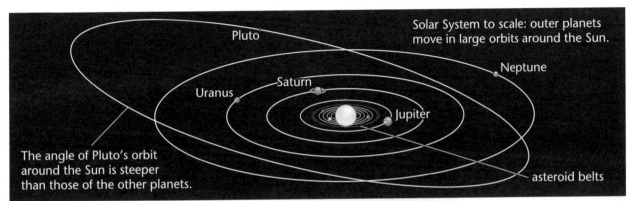

Solar System to scale: outer planets move in large orbits around the Sun.

The angle of Pluto's orbit around the Sun is steeper than those of the other planets.

Each planet takes a different time to make one complete orbit of the Sun. The time it takes to do this is called a year. The Earth takes a non-whole number ($365\frac{1}{4}$) of Earth days to make its orbit. We have to add an extra 'leap' day to our calendar every four years (in a leap year) to allow for the extra $\frac{1}{4}$ day in each year.

A good way of remembering the names of the planets in the right order is to use the first letter of each name to make words in a sentence that is easy to remember. (This kind of sentence is called a mnemonic.) Here is a mnemonic which may help you.

My **V**ery **E**asy **M**ethod **J**ust **S**hows **U**s **N**ames of **P**lanets

1 Draw a diagram of the Sun. Label it with important facts about its key features.

2 What is the main difference between a star and a planet?

3 Use the first letters of the nine planets to write your own mnemonic to help you learn their names in the right order.

4 Explain what would happen if we did not add a 'leap' day once every four years to our calendar.

Fascinating planet facts

All the planets in our solar system orbit the Sun. The four inner planets nearest to the Sun are relatively small and rocky. All of the others, except Pluto, are much larger and mostly made of gas. Some planets can be seen with the naked eye. More have been found as ways of looking into outer space have improved.

The four inner planets

Mercury, Venus and Mars have been seen with the naked eye since ancient times. Our knowledge about them has increased since the USSR space probe *Venera 7* was first sent to Venus in 1970 and *Mars 3* to Mars in 1971. In 1974 the American probe, *US Mariner 10*, sent back the first pictures of the surface of Mercury.

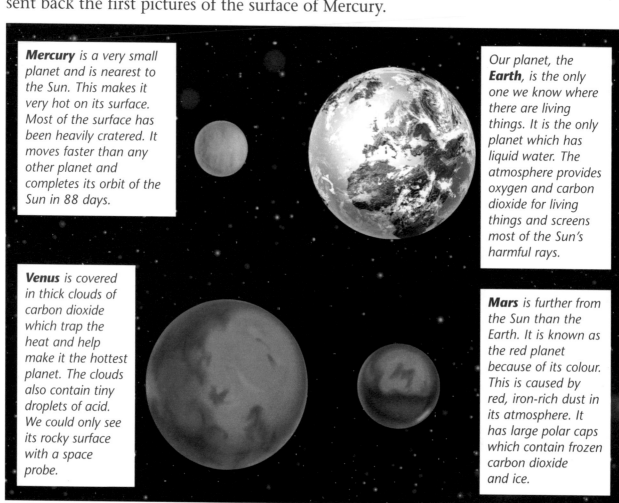

Mercury is a very small planet and is nearest to the Sun. This makes it very hot on its surface. Most of the surface has been heavily cratered. It moves faster than any other planet and completes its orbit of the Sun in 88 days.

Our planet, the **Earth**, is the only one we know where there are living things. It is the only planet which has liquid water. The atmosphere provides oxygen and carbon dioxide for living things and screens most of the Sun's harmful rays.

Venus is covered in thick clouds of carbon dioxide which trap the heat and help make it the hottest planet. The clouds also contain tiny droplets of acid. We could only see its rocky surface with a space probe.

Mars is further from the Sun than the Earth. It is known as the red planet because of its colour. This is caused by red, iron-rich dust in its atmosphere. It has large polar caps which contain frozen carbon dioxide and ice.

The five outer planets

Beyond the orbit of Mars lie the five outer planets. Both Jupiter and Saturn have been known for a long time but the invention of telescopes showed that they both have moons and that Saturn has a fantastic set of rings around its equator. Careful sky watching, better telescopes and scientific prediction of where the next planet might be found led to the discovery of Uranus in 1738, Neptune in 1845 and Pluto in 1932.

Jupiter is the biggest (it could contain 1300 Earths) and fastest spinning planet in our solar system. You can see its great red spot, its polar regions and belts. Its atmosphere contains hydrogen and helium. It is very cold.

Uranus is the third largest planet. It is also made of hydrogen and helium: a little methane gas gives it its green colour. It looks very featureless through a telescope. It is dimly lit and orbited by 15 moons and a set of rings. The seasons at its poles last for 42 years.

Saturn's atmosphere is mostly very cold hydrogen gas. It is almost as big as Jupiter and has a thin wide set of rings. Their diameter is about the same as the distance between the Earth and the Moon.

Neptune is made of the same gases as Uranus and also has a set of rings. It is extremely cold. The winds in its atmosphere are the fastest in the solar system. Its great dark spot is as big as the Earth.

Pluto is the smallest, darkest and coldest planet. It is made of ice and methane.

1 Find out some more fascinating facts about the nine planets. Think of an impressive way to present your findings to your friends.

2 Make up a quiz about the nine planets. Test it out on your class.

3 Explain the major differences between the inner and the outer planets.

4 Design a brochure which illustrates the main features of one of the planets in the solar system.

I see the Moon

The Moon orbits the Earth once every 28.3 days (one lunar month). The Moon does not make its own light. You only see it because it reflects light from the Sun into your eyes. At different times in its orbit you can see different amounts of its surface lit by the Sun. We call these views the phases of the Moon.

What causes the phases of the Moon?

Michelle is a keen astronomer and is finding out more about the **Moon**. As she looks into the night sky she can see part of the Moon's surface lit up by the Sun. The amount she sees changes from day to day.

Sun

If the Moon is here you can see part of it.

If the Moon is here then none of the light from the Sun can be reflected to you.

Earth

These changing views are called the **phases of the Moon.** They are caused because of the way the Sun, the Earth and the Moon are lined up in Space.

What does Michelle see each night?

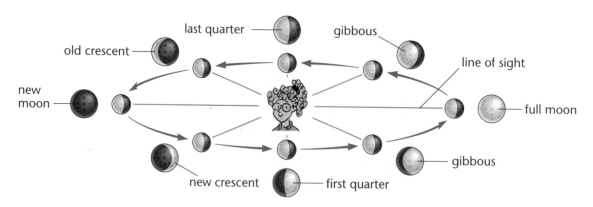

▲ *Phases of the Moon. The inner circle of pictures shows what the Moon would look like from space. The outer circle shows what Michelle can see.*

When the Moon is furthest away from the Sun in its orbit Michelle sees it all lit up. This is called a full Moon. When it is closest to the Sun Michelle sees a new Moon: it is not lit up at all. When the Moon is half way between these two phases then Michelle sees about half of it lit up. These phases are called the first and last quarters.

How do lunar and solar eclipses happen?

Sometimes the Sun, the Earth and the Moon line up exactly so that the Earth's shadow passes across the Moon. This is called a **lunar eclipse**. Each time this happens it can be seen at a different place on the Earth. If Michelle were lucky enough she might see the Earth's shadow blocking out part of the light hitting the Moon.

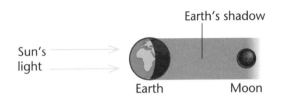

▲ *We cannot see the parts of the Moon which are passing through the Earth's shadow.*

At other times the Sun, Earth and the Moon line up so exactly that the Moon casts a small shadow on the Earth. This is known as a **solar eclipse**. Even though the Sun is very much larger than the Moon, it is so much further away that they look almost the same size in the sky. This is why the Moon looks as if it is covering the Sun.

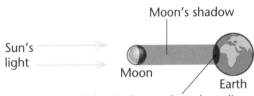

This part of the Earth sees the solar eclipse.

What can Michelle see when she looks closely at the Moon?

As she looked at the Moon Michelle was really puzzled about why the same side of the Moon always faces the Earth. The reason is that the Moon takes the same time to orbit the Earth as it takes to make one complete turn on its axis. So the same part of the Moon always faces the Earth.

Michelle sees craters which were formed by large meteors hitting the surface many years ago. There are also mountains and plains which used, wrongly, to be called seas.

1 Using your own words and diagrams explain why you see the different phases of the Moon.

2 If the Moon had its own light, what would it look like each night of the month?

The Earth, the Sun and the Moon

The Sun is much bigger than the Earth. The Sun is a star. It is closer to the Earth than it is to other stars. The Moon is smaller than the Earth and closer than the Sun. The Moon orbits the Earth. The Earth, the Sun and the Moon are all round or ball-shaped.

What do we know about the Sun?

On clear days the Sun shines brightly in the sky. It is so bright because it is made from very hot gases. It looks small because it is a long way from us. In fact, it is very big, much bigger than Earth.

Earth

.

▲ *If the Earth was this size …*

Sun

… the Sun would be ten times bigger than this.

▲ *Can you see this many stars on a clear night?*

On a clear night you can see lots of **stars**. They are just like our Sun but much further away. Our Sun is just one of the millions of stars.

Some stars are too far away to be seen clearly. You can only see these with binoculars or a telescope.

Galileo, who lived about 400 years ago, was the first scientist to study the Sun. He went blind from looking at it for too long. We now know it is very dangerous to look directly at the Sun.

All living things need light and heat from the Sun to grow.

What do we know about the Moon?

The Moon is moving in an orbit round the Earth. Sometimes we can see the Moon during the day if the sky is clear. At other times we see the Moon at night.

The Moon is easier to see at night because the sky is dark.

When you look at the Moon you will see it has dark patches on its surface. These are craters or huge holes up to 250 kilometres across.

The shape of the Earth, the Sun and the Moon

▲ *The Earth and Moon seen from space.*

People used to believe that the Earth was flat. We now know that the Sun, the Moon and the Earth are all spherical like balls. Astronauts can see the shapes of the Earth and Moon from their spacecraft.

1 Read the information about the Sun. Now write three sentences of facts about the Sun. Add more if you can.

2 Which is nearer to the Earth – the Sun or the Moon?

3 When can you see the Moon? Is it only at night-time?

4 Draw a diagram of what the Sun, the Moon and the Earth would look like seen from a spaceship.

Movements of the Sun

The Sun rises in the east and sets in the west. The Sun does not move but the Earth does. It spins like a top or turns on its own axis. The Earth completes one rotation every 24 hours. It also travels round the Sun taking a year to complete an orbit.

What happens to the Sun during the day?

When you get up in the morning, the Sun is in the east.

By midday the Sun is in the south but higher in the sky. In the evening the Sun sets in the west.

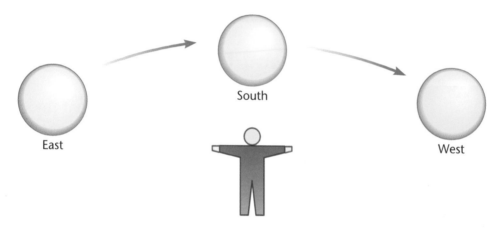

It seems that the Sun is moving around the Earth. For many years everyone believed that was what happened. Now we know that the Earth is moving, and not the Sun. The Earth is spinning like a top. Each day it turns a full **rotation**.

The Sun rises in the east as the Earth turns towards the Sun.

At midday the Sun will be facing you. In the evening the Sun sets in the west as the Earth turns away from the Sun into darkness.

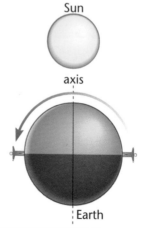

What happens when the Sun sets?

As the Earth turns away from the Sun, the Sun disappears over the horizon. You may see some beautiful colours when the Sun is low in the sky.

How does the Earth move?

As well as turning on its own **axis**, the Earth is also moving round the Sun. It takes one year for it to complete a full cycle. The scientist, Sir Isaac Newton, explained how gravity holds the Earth in orbit round the Sun.

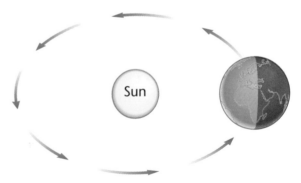

▲ *One orbit takes a year.*

1 From which direction does the Sun rise? In which direction does it set?

2 The Sun appears to be moving across the sky. Explain in your own words why this is not really what is happening.

3 How long does it take for the Earth to turn once on its axis?

4 How long does it take for the Earth to orbit the Sun?

Day and night

When the Sun lights up our part of the Earth it is our daytime. At night the Sun no longer shines on our part of the Earth. This will be our night-time. When it is our daytime it will be night-time on the opposite side of the Earth.

When do we have daytime?

When the Sun rises, light falls on our part of the Earth. This is our **day-time**. As the Earth turns, the Sun continues to light up the sky. When it is dull the Sun's rays still spread light through the clouds.

person in daylight

▲ *It will be daylight for the part of the Earth facing the Sun.*

As the Sun sets the sky will get darker. Even when the Sun can no longer be seen, its rays continue to light up the sky. As the Earth turns further away from the Sun, the sky becomes dark. While it is **night-time** in our part of the Earth, it will be daylight on the other side of the Earth.

person in the night

▲ *It will be night-time for the part of the Earth facing away from the Sun.*

At night-time no light from the Sun reaches us. Darkness is the absence of light.

Why is a day 24 hours long?

The Earth spins around its axis once a day or about every 24 hours. The length of one day is the same for every point on the Earth.

Why is the length of daylight shorter in winter?

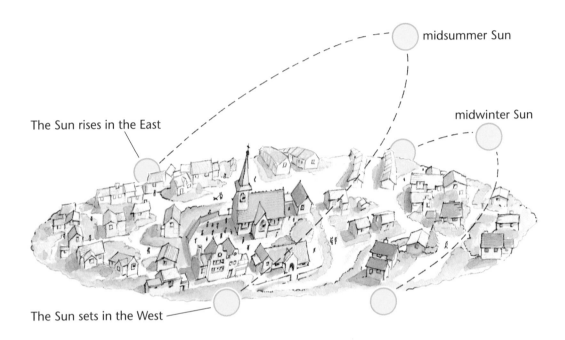

midsummer Sun

midwinter Sun

The Sun rises in the East

The Sun sets in the West

Because the Earth is tilted, in different seasons the Sun reaches different heights in the sky in Britain. This changes the length of daylight.

In winter the path of the Sun is low in the sky and only above the horizon for a few hours. The 'days are shorter'. At midsummer the Sun is at its highest point in the sky. The Sun is above the horizon for longer and the 'days are longer'.

On the shortest day in Britain you can expect only about 6 hours of daylight. On the longest day it is close to $16\frac{1}{2}$ hours.

Further north the length of daylight in winter is even shorter and in summer longer. The North pole has 24 hours of darkness in winter and 24 hours of daylight in summer.

1 Explain what is meant by day, night and the Earth's axis.

2 Explain why we have more daylight hours during the summer than in winter in Britain.

The Moon

The Moon is moving round the Earth. It takes 28 days to complete one cycle. The Moon reflects light from the Sun. The shape of the Moon appears to change. This depends on how much of the sunlit surface we see.

What do we know about the Moon's movements?

The Moon is in orbit round the Earth. It takes 28 days for the Moon to orbit the Earth. Our word 'month' comes from the word 'moon'.

▲ It takes 28 days for the Moon to orbit the Earth.

The Moon also turns on its own axis once every 28 days. This means that the same side of the Moon always faces Earth.

We found out what the other side was like only when spacecraft travelled round the Moon. As scientists had expected, it is much the same as the side we can see.

Does the Moon shine?

The Moon is not like a star. It is made from rocks, not hot gases. It is not like the Sun giving out heat and light. It only *appears* to shine because it is *reflecting* light from the Sun.

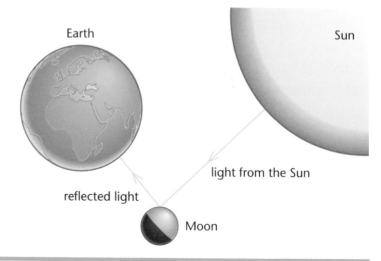

Earth

Sun

light from the Sun

reflected light

Moon

Why does the Moon appear to change shape?

You may have noticed that sometimes the Moon looks circular. This is a full moon. At other times it may be a half moon or a **crescent**. Its shape depends on how much of its surface we see lit by the Sun.

For part of the month the Moon cannot be seen from Earth. This is when the Moon is between the Earth and the Sun. This is called a new moon.

Jack decided he would keep a diary of the shape of the Moon for four weeks. Each day he looked for the Moon and drew a picture of its shape.

He found that during the four weeks its shape changed from a new moon to a crescent, then to a half moon, then to a full moon and back again.

Day 1	Day 3	Day 7	Day 15	Day 21	Day 24	Day 28
new moon	crescent	half moon	full moon	half moon	crescent	new moon

Jack found that each **lunar month** the Moon goes through a cycle when its shape appears to change. We call these the **phases** of the Moon.

If you watch the Moon for a day you will find that, like the Sun, it rises in the east and sets in the west.

1 If you were on the Moon what would it look like?

2 How long does it take for the Moon to orbit the Earth?

3 From which direction does the Moon rise and where does it set?

4 Explain in your own words why the Moon's shape appears to change during the month.

5 How does the Moon shine?

The four seasons

Places on the Earth that are not near the equator have four seasons. Because the Earth is tilted one pole or the other is pointed towards the Sun as it moves in its orbit. When the North pole is pointing towards the Sun it is summer north of the equator and people living in the south have winter.

What causes the four seasons?

Our Earth makes one complete orbit around the Sun every year. The tilt of the Earth's axis causes the seasons because in summer we have more hours of sunlight and in winter the nights are longer. So in summer there is more time for everything to get warmer.

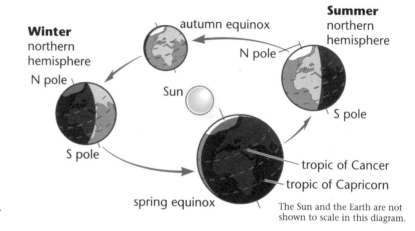

Winter
northern
hemisphere
N pole

S pole

autumn equinox

N pole

Sun

spring equinox

Summer
northern
hemisphere

S pole

tropic of Cancer

tropic of Capricorn

The Sun and the Earth are not shown to scale in this diagram.

What happens at the winter and summer solstices?

In Britain the shortest day happens on or about December 21st. This is called the winter **solstice**.

On this day the Sun is directly over the tropic of Capricorn and the North pole points away from the Sun. In Britain the Sun is low in the sky and gives little sunlight.

On or about June 21st the Earth has moved half way around its orbit. This is the day when we have the most hours of daylight and is the summer **solstice** or midsummer.

On this day the Sun is directly over the tropic of Cancer and the North pole points towards the Sun. In Britain the Sun is high in the sky and we get a lot of sunlight.

What happens at the spring and autumn equinoxes?

The other two important days in the year are on or about March 21st and September 21st. These dates fall midway between the solstices.

On both of these days the Sun shines directly over the equator and neither of the two poles faces towards the Sun. In Britain the Sun is at its mid-height in the sky.

As March 21st approaches the length of daylight has been getting longer. On this day the length of daylight and night-time are the same. This is called an **equinox**.

A second equinox occurs on September 21st. During the summer there has been more than 12 hours of daylight. It shortens to 12 hours exactly on this day.

Are the times of the seasons the same in New Zealand?

New Zealand is similar to Britain but is on the other side of the world. Britain is about as far north from the equator as New Zealand is south.

When it is midwinter in England it is about midsummer in New Zealand. Do you fancy spending Christmas Day on the beach?

1 Explain what is special about 21st December and June 21st each year.

2 Explain what is special about 21st March and September 22nd each year.

3 Between which days each year are the days getting longer? Between which days do they get shorter?

4 Use diagrams to help you describe how the seasons would change if you lived in New Zealand.

5 What would happen to the length of daylight and night-time if the Earth was not tilted as it orbited the Sun?

Test your knowledge

1 Use the words from the list to fill in the spaces below. Write out the complete paragraph neatly in your book with the correct words added. Underline them carefully.

The .... is one of nine planets which circle the Sun to form what we call the .... system. The Sun is a very hot .... and is at the middle. A non-stop nuclear explosion inside it releases huge amounts of heat and light. Dark .... are often found on its surface. The four .... and rocky planets are called Mercury, ... , Earth and .... The five outer planets, with the exception of Pluto and are mainly made from .... Their names are Jupiter, ... , Uranus, ... and Pluto.

**inner   Saturn   Earth   gas
Solar   star   Venus   Mars
sunspots   Neptune**

Now look through this chapter and try to find the best words to fill the spaces. Copy out the paragraph in your book with the spaces filled with the best words.

The planets move around the Sun in .... The Earth takes $365\frac{1}{4}$ days to .... the Sun. This length of time is called one .... The Earth .... around once every day and brings .... and .... If you are on the part of the Earth which .... the Sun you will see daylight.

2 Start with two fresh pages in your book. Draw a circle which shows how big each planet is. You will need compasses, a ruler and a pencil. The diameter of each circle is given below. On this scale each 1 cm you use equals 10 000 km in real life.

Mercury = 0.5 cm   Venus = 1.2 cm
Earth = 1.3 cm   Mars = 0.7 cm
Jupiter = 14.3 cm   Saturn = 12 cm
Uranus = 5.2 cm   Neptune = 5 cm
Pluto = 0.2 cm

Use this and other books to draw, colour and label the surface markings on each planet such as rings, polar caps, coloured clouds or craters. Make your drawings as accurate as possible.

3 A visitor has arrived from another planet. She wants to know what causes night and day and the four seasons. Write down the conversation you have with her to explain this. If you have time, turn your work into a cartoon strip for a children's comic.

4 Use your nearest library and an encyclopaedia or CD-ROM to find out more about the exploration of space by the USA and USSR. Design a time line which shows what has happened from the time the first satellite was put into Space until now.

Changing sounds

Before you start you should know that:
- there are many kinds of sound and many sources
- sounds travel away from sources, getting fainter as they do so
- you hear sounds when they enter your ear

At the start of this unit you will learn about vibrations and:
- how sounds are produced
- what materials sound can travel through
- what happens if sounds are too loud
- how we can stop sound from reaching our ears

Later in the unit you will learn more about changing sounds and:
- how to make sounds loud and soft
- what sound waves look like
- how to alter pitch
- what is meant by amplitude and frequency

How sound travels

You hear many different sounds every day. Sound, like light, is a form of energy. Sounds are caused by vibrations. You hear sounds when these vibrations travel to your ears. Sound travels well through some materials and not so well through others. Sound travels much more slowly than light.

What are sounds?

Sounds are produced when objects vibrate. These vibrating objects are called **sound sources**.

You already know many sound sources. The picture shows some of them. You can talk, shout and sing because your vocal cords vibrate inside your throat.

When you drop a stone into a pool of water, **vibrations** or ripples travel outwards as miniature **waves**.

In the same way, sound energy from a source travels outwards in all directions. You hear the sounds because vibrations are carried as **sound waves** in the air to your ears.

What else can sound travel through?

Sound does not just travel in the air, it can travel through different materials:

- sound travels best through hard, solid materials
- sound travels quite well through liquids
- sound travels poorly in gases such as air.

Sound does *not* travel at all in a vacuum. In space it is silent!

Some materials can prevent sound travelling. They are called **insulators**. We can use these materials to protect our ears or help prevent noise pollution.

At sports day, if you are far away from the starting line, you may see the smoke from the starting pistol *before* you hear the bang. This is because light travels faster than sound.

This also explains why you usually see aeroplanes before you hear them and why, during a storm, you usually see the lightning before you hear the thunder.

1 What makes the vibrations in each of the sound sources in the first picture?

2 Draw a picture to show how sound travels from a firework to your ears.

3 The crew of the Space Shuttle can hear each other talking, their radio and their own engine. Which materials in the Shuttle allow sound to travel the best? Which would be the worst?

4 When might we want to protect our ears from some sounds?

5 If you are close to a bolt of lightning the thunder and lightning come together. Why do we see the lightning first if we are a long way away?

6 Name a passenger aeroplane which travels faster than sound.

Hearing sound

Sound can be heard when it enters our ears. Inside each ear is an ear drum which vibrates when sound vibrations hit it. Very loud sounds can damage the delicate parts inside the ear. Sometimes it is important to protect the ears from loud noises. We can do this with a material which is good for sound proofing.

Can loud music damage your ears?

Michelle plays her music very loudly! Tom is not happy.

Michelle is wrong. Very loud music can damage your ears.

The shape of your outer ear helps to trap the sound and carry it into your ear. The important parts of your ear are inside your skull so they cannot be damaged easily.

Sound waves enter your ear and make the **ear drum** vibrate. Very loud music can damage the delicate parts inside your ear.

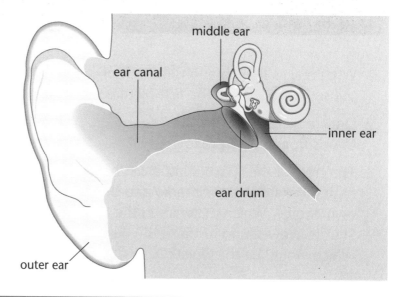

How can we block out sound?

Ear muffs muffle sound so that loud noise cannot reach the ear drum. Ear muffs cover up your ears. It is dangerous to push things inside your ear because it might damage the ear drum.

▲ *Sand bags also muffle sound.*

Which material is good for sound insulation?

Michelle was asked to find the best material to use for ear muffs. She stood a radio on a table and turned it on. She pressed different materials to her ears and listened. She tried to decide how well she could hear the radio. She put her results into a table.

material	can hear
sponge rubber	
carpet	
bubble wrap	
egg box	

1 Suggest some places where the noise could be so loud that it could damage your ears.

2 What are people advised to do if they work where there is a loud noise?

3 Do you think Michelle has designed a fair test? Make a list of ways in which you think she could improve this investigation.

4 Make a list of materials that you think would be useful to use for sound insulation.

105

Loud and soft

Sounds travelling from a source can vary in loudness. The loudness of a sound depends upon the size of the vibrations making the sound. Loud sounds carry more energy than quiet sounds. Their sound waves have a bigger amplitude.

Musical instruments can be played quietly or loudly. This is how you can make the music more interesting.

Mina's class were investigating loud and soft sounds. She was twanging a ruler on the edge of her desk.

Yasmin and Tom were banging a drum. It had rice on it. The drum skin vibrated and made the rice jump up and down.

The children discovered that if they twanged the ruler or banged the drum hard, the vibrations were bigger. They thought that this made the sound louder.

What do sounds look like?

You cannot *see* sounds, of course, but you can use patterns to help you understand more about sound. (These patterns can be shown on a special device called an **oscilloscope**.) Some patterns are shown below.

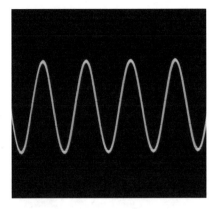

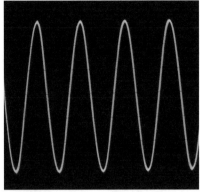

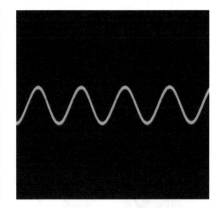

This pattern shows that vibrations travel as **sound waves**.

This is a pattern for *loud* sounds. They have *tall waves* and *large vibrations*.

This is a pattern for *soft* sounds. They have *small waves* and *small vibrations*.

(Not all sound waves are smooth like these.)

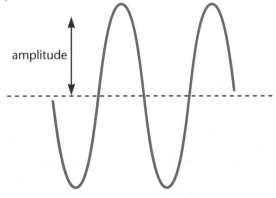

The height of the sound wave is called its **amplitude**.

The *bigger* the *amplitude*, the *louder* the *sound*.

---

1 Imagine people playing a drum, a flute, a guitar and a xylophone. How would you make each instrument play louder and softer?

2 Use page 150 of the Glossary to find out what an oscilloscope does, and the meaning of the word amplitude.

3 Draw one oscilloscope pattern for a loud note and another one for a soft note.

4 How are vibrations from a loud sound different to those from a soft sound?

5 How is the amplitude of a loud sound different to that of a soft sound?

High and low

Sounds from a source can vary in pitch. Pitch is how high or low a noise sounds. Slow vibrations produce low notes or sounds. Fast vibrations produce high notes or sounds. The sound waves of high and low notes have different frequencies.

Matthew's class were investigating high notes and low notes. They were using different things to do the investigation.

▲ The shorter the 'squeaker', the higher the note.

▲ Bottles with more water made lower notes.

Sara and Jack were investigating a guitar. Jack noticed that when the vibrating part of the string was *shorter*, the **pitch** of the note produced was *higher*.

Sara looked carefully and saw that the strings producing *low* pitched notes seemed to vibrate a little more *slowly* than the ones producing higher pitched notes.

Sara and Jack decided that the *faster the vibration*, the *higher the pitch of the note*. They looked at the other investigations to try and test their idea. They could not see the speed of the vibrations.

More sound patterns

Here are more sound patterns to help you understand different sounds.
(These patterns were made with an oscilloscope like those on page 107.)

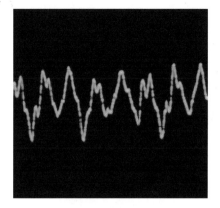 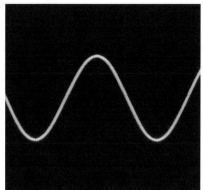 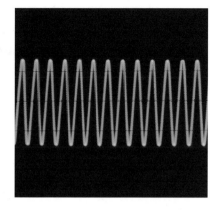

This pattern shows that different instruments give different patterns.
This shows us why they *sound* different.

This pattern shows that *low* notes have waves which are *spread out*.
This means that the vibrations are *slow*.

This pattern shows that waves of *high* notes are *close together*.
This means that the vibrations are *fast*.

The length of each vibration is called the **wavelength** of the sound. This is always a very, very small number.

The number of vibrations in one second is called the **frequency** of the sound. The higher the frequency, the higher the pitch of the note.

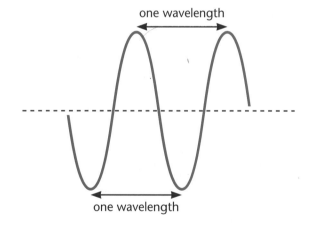

one wavelength

one wavelength

1 How could you change the pitch of the instruments used by the children?

2 Use page 150 of the Glossary to find the meaning of these words: pitch, frequency, wavelength.

3 Why do different instruments not sound the same if they are playing the same notes?

4 Draw one oscilloscope pattern for a high note and another for a low note.

5 How are the vibrations of a high note different to those of a low note?

Test your knowledge

1 Make a word-search containing some or all of these words or phrases. Add some more words about sound.

**vibration   pitch   frequency
amplitude   loud   soft
high   wavelength**

2 Use words from the list below to fill in the spaces. Write out the passage in your book with the correct words added.

Guitar strings .... and make sounds. Loud notes are made by .... the strings .... The guitar can be played .... by plucking the strings softly. When the strings are plucked harder, the .... of the vibrations is made .... When a guitar is played quietly, the amplitude of the .... is ....

**vibrations   larger   smaller
quietly   vibrate   plucking
hard   amplitude**

3 Write a letter to your pen-friend in Australia. Tell them how you can use an oscilloscope to learn about sound. Draw pictures for them and use these words in your letter.

**pitch   high   low   notes
sound waves   frequency
wavelength   vibrations
fast   slow**

4
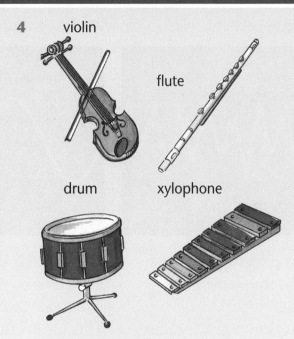
violin

flute

drum   xylophone

These are all pictures of musical instruments. For each instrument say what is vibrating to make the sound and how the pitch of the note can be changed.

5 Close your eyes and listen very carefully. Make a list of all the sounds that you can hear.

All about forces

Before you start you should know that:

- forces cause pushes, pulls or turns
- some everyday forces are large, others are small
- gravity is a force that pulls objects towards the centre of the Earth
- forces can be measured in units of newtons (N) using a newton meter
- all forces have a size and act in a particular direction
- friction is a force that slows down objects as they move
- air resistance and water resistance are types of friction

In this unit you will learn more about forces in action and that:

- the Earth and objects are pulled towards each other and this causes the object to have weight
- weight is a force and is measured in units of newtons
- mass is different from weight and many people get these confused
- newton meters are used to measure the size of everyday forces
- several forces can act on an object at the same time
- when an object is in water, the water provides an upward force called upthrust on it which makes the object feel lighter than it does in air
- elastic bands or springs stretch more as more weights are added because the downward pull caused by gravity acting on the weights increases
- air resistance slows down objects which move through air

The special force of gravity

Earth's gravity pulls objects towards the centre of the Earth and gives them weight. Weight is a force that is measured in newtons (N). Other planets also have gravity but the size of the gravity may be different from on Earth. Objects weight more where the gravity is bigger.

What do we know about gravity?

Gravity is an invisible force. It holds you onto the Earth. It speeds you up as you cycle downhill and pulls you back as you go uphill. It makes everything fall to the ground. It holds the atmosphere in place, the Moon in its orbit around the Earth and the Earth in orbit around the Sun. You cannot see it, but you can observe its effects.

▲ *Can you spot ten examples of gravity in action?*

Gravity is a *pulling* force. It is easiest to see with large objects like our Earth.

Gravity always pulls, it never pushes. The pull is always in a straight line, it never turns. On Earth the size of this pull is almost the same wherever you go.

When an apple falls off a tree the Earth's gravity pulls it downwards. It falls in a straight line, as if it were heading towards the centre of the Earth.

If you took the same apple much further away, say as far as the Moon, the gravity would still pull on the apple – but the pull would be smaller in size.

The difference between Jack's mass and weight

Like all objects Jack has **mass**. This tells you how much material is in his body. It is measured in grams (g) or in kilograms (kg).

The idea of mass is often confused with **weight**. Jack also has weight. This tells you how strongly the force of gravity is pulling on Jack's mass. Weight is a force and is measured in newtons (N).

On Earth every kilogram of mass is pulled down by gravity with a force of 10 N.

▲ *Jack has a mass of 40 kg and a weight of 400 N on the Earth.*

What happens to Jack's mass and weight on the Moon?

The mass of an object never changes no matter where you take it.

If Jack could travel to the Moon *his mass* (40 kg) *would be the same* as it is on Earth. He still contains the same amount of material.

An object's weight will change if you take it to where the force of gravity is different.

If Jack could travel to the Moon he would find that *his weight changes*. The Moon's pull is one-sixth that of the Earth.

▲ *Jack's mass on the Moon is 40 kg: his weight is 67 N.*

1 Write down all the ways in which you can spot gravity working in the picture on the opposite page.

2 Think of five different ways in which gravity has affected you today. Write an interesting sentence about each of these.

3 Explain in your own words the difference between mass and weight.

4 Jupiter has a gravity pull which is $2\frac{1}{2}$ times bigger than the Earth's. Use the ideas on this page to work out Jack's weight on Jupiter. Make sure you use the correct units.

Force diagrams

You can always find out how big a force is and in what direction it is acting. You have to know both to describe it accurately. Force diagrams are drawn to show both the *size* and *direction* of a force. The length of the line drawn to scale shows the size of the force. The way in which it points shows its direction.

How can you describe a force well?

Two things about a **force** are important. They are:

- the direction of the force;
- the size of the force.

You can draw lines with arrowheads to show the size and direction of forces. The way the arrow points shows the *direction* of the force. The length of the line shows its *size*.

However, you have to draw the length to scale to help you work out its size. You should always show the scale that you are using.

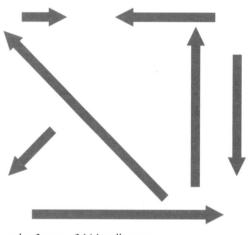

scale: 1 cm = 1 N in all cases

A simple force diagram

A **force diagram** shows the forces which are acting on an object. Each force is drawn as a separate arrow that shows the direction and size of the force.

Think about a football when it is still. It has two forces acting on it. The force of gravity pulls it down, but the ground gives it an equal force in an upwards direction.

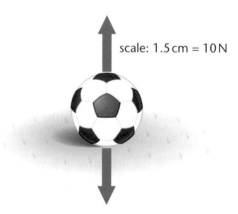

scale: 1.5 cm = 10 N

These forces are *equal* in size and act in *opposite* directions. As a result the football does not move. The forces are balanced and no movement takes place.

A force diagram can be drawn to show this. The length of the lines are drawn to a chosen scale. Each arrow points in the direction of a force.

A more complicated diagram

Think about another football being kicked forward. There are four different forces acting on it.

Force 1 is the large kicking force which pushes the football forwards.

Force 2 is a small air resistance force which acts in the opposite direction to the kicking force.

Force 3 is the force of gravity which pulls the ball down. This is the weight of the ball.

Force 4 comes from the ground. This acts in the opposite direction to gravity and pushes the ball with a force which is equal to its weight.

In the force diagram you will see that the length of the lines tells you about the size of each force The arrows show you the direction in which each force is acting.

1 Measure the arrows in the top diagram on page 114. What forces are they measuring? (Don't forget to state their size and direction.)

2 Draw lines to show forces which are 10 N, 25 N, 42 N and 50 N in size. Remember to choose and mark a good scale.

3 Draw the same lines pointing in four different directions. Underneath each line describe in your own words what the line tells you about the size and direction of each force.

4 Explain in your own words what is meant by:

  a a scale   b a force diagram
  c opposite forces   d gravity.

Forces in water

More than one force can act on an object at the same time. You can measure the force of gravity on an object using a newton meter. This is the weight of the object. If you put the same object in water it will weigh less because the water tries to push it up. The upwards push (called the upthrust) balances some of the weight.

How much does Jack weigh?

Jack weighs himself every week. He is growing fast and is keeping track of his weight. He weighs 400 newtons (N) on the scales when he weighs himself in air.

But when he goes to the swimming pool he feels lighter in the water. When his feet are off the bottom of the pool he starts to float. This is because water pushes him upwards with a force called **upthrust**.

What forces act on Jack when he swims?

Several forces act on Jack when he swims.

Each acts in a particular direction and has a certain size.

▲ If you could weigh Jack in water with a large newton meter he would weigh less than he does in air.

His flippers give him a force which moves him forward.

As he pushes through water he finds there is another force. Water resistance tries to stop him moving forward.

The water also exerts a force that tries to push him upwards. This is called upthrust. It cancels out some of the downward force due to gravity.

Measuring upthrust with a newton meter

Jack decided to try to measure how much lighter some objects were when he put them in water. Here are some of his notes.

I tried to find out the upthrust on some objects when they are put in water. This is the force pushing upwards on an object in water. It comes from the push of the water. I filled a big bowl three-quarters full of water. I also had a newton meter which weighed objects up to 10 N, and some objects to weigh. First of all I weighed each of the objects in air with the newton meter. I wrote their weights in a table. I expected each one to weigh less in water, just like I do when I go swimming. Then I weighed them all again when they were in water. The upthrust of the water balanced some of the weight. To work out the upthrust I subtracted the weight of the each object in water from its weight in air.

Upthrust = weight of object in air – weight of the object in water

	Stone	Marble	Wood	Metal	Plastic toy
Weight in air (N)	4	2	7	10	3
Weight in water (N)	3	1.5	5	7	2.5

1 What four forces act on Jack when he goes swimming?

2 Where does the force of gravity try to pull Jack?

3 Where does the upthrust force try to push Jack?

4 Work out the upthrust for each object Jack put into water.

Newton meters

Forces are measured in units of newtons (N) using a newton meter. Weight is a force so it is also measured in newtons. The newton meter has a calibrated scale with markings which are equally spaced. This lets you measure any force whose size is between the smallest and largest marking on the scale.

What is inside a newton meter?

A newton meter contains a stretchy spring. When an object is attached to the spring, gravity pulls downwards on the object and makes the spring longer.

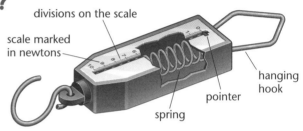

The more mass the object has, the bigger the gravity and the more the spring stretches. If you double the pulling force the spring will double in length.

How do you calibrate the scale?

Mina calibrated a newton meter which could measure forces up to 1 N. She added small weights one at a time, marking the **scale** every time a new one had been added.

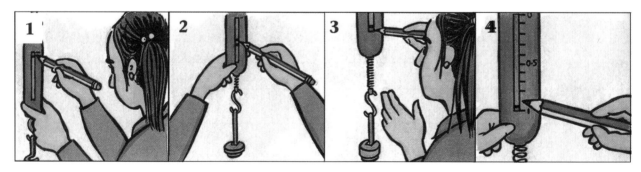

1 When there is no pull, the spring is not stretched. Mina marks the top of the scale with 0 N.

2 She adds 0.5 N weight. The spring stretches a little. Mina makes a second mark accurately half way down the scale.

3 A 1 N weight stretches the spring twice as far. Mina marks this point on the scale 1 N.

4 Mina makes more marks by dividing the total length into ten equal parts. Each division measures an extra 0.1 N.

Measuring

Mina decided to see how the length of a spring inside a newton meter changed as she added more weights. She added 10 N weights one by one to her newton meter which could measure up to 100 N. She put her results in a table and then plotted a line graph of her results.

Weight which is added to the newton meter (N)	0	10	20	30	40	50	60	70	80	90	100
Length of the spring (cm)	0	1	4	6	9	10	12	13	17	18	20

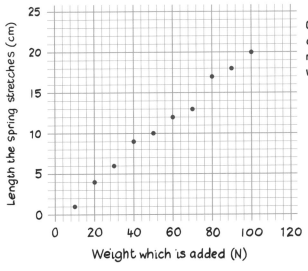

Graph to show how the length of a spring in a Newton meter changes as more weights are added.

1 Describe in your own words how you would calibrate a newton meter.

2 Explain why a newton meter, which can measure up to 10 N has a stronger spring inside it than one which can measure up to 1 N.

3 Draw four pictures of newton meters measuring the forces of 0.75 N, 0.8 N, 0.25 N and 0.2 N.

4 Look carefully at Mina's graph. Plot it out yourself on some graph paper.

a On which axis did she put 'what she changed'?

b On which axis did she put 'what she measured'?

c Which results do not quite fit?

d Why?

e What does the graph tell you about how the length of a spring changes as you add more weights?

Falling spinners

An object which falls through the air is pulled towards the Earth by gravity. As it falls down the force of air resistance pushes against the direction of movement of the object and balances out some of the force pulling it down. This makes the object fall more slowly. The bigger the air resistance, the slower the object will fall.

What forces act on a falling spinner?

Sycamore seeds are designed to fall from the tree and spin a long distance away. This gives them a better chance of finding a good place to grow. The seed has two 'wings' and is carefully weighted and balanced. A paper spinner can be designed in the same way. When they fall, the seed and the spinner have two main forces acting on them. The force of gravity acts downwards and the force of air resistance acts upwards. They fall because the downward pull of gravity is bigger than the upward force of air resistance.

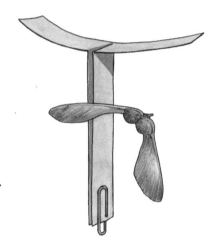

Investigating how fast spinners fall

Mr Smith's class investigated how fast different paper spinners fell to the ground. They each did a fair test and their results are on the next page.

Talking about the results

Group 1: We made five spinners with a different number of paper clips on each one. We dropped each spinner from the same height. It was hard for Jack to judge the exact time of fall on many of the tests as the falling time was so short. So we repeated the measurements so that we could work out an average result for each test.

Number of paper clips on the spinner	1	2	3	4	5
Time taken to fall (s)	1.0 1.2 0.9 0.9	0.9 0.9 0.7 0.75	0.8 0.65 0.63 0.63	0.7 0.75 0.47 0.45	0.62 0.64 0.23 0.25

Group 2: Our test worked really well. We used the same spinner each time and just varied the height we dropped it. The higher we dropped the spinner the longer it took to fall to the ground, just as we predicted it would. We did each test two times because we found that the results were quite close each time.

Height of fall (m)	2.0	1.75	1.5	1.25	1.0
Time taken to fall (s)	5.1 5.2	4.5 4.5	3.9 4.1	3.55 3.45	3.0 3.1

Group 3: We dropped our spinners from the same height each time but changed the length of the wings. We had to add some plasticine to the spinners as we made each wing shorter so that the weight of each spinner was the same. As they fell they took a little time to start spinning. But as they picked up speed they spun faster and this made them fly better. We only had time to take one reading for each spinner.

Length of wing (cm)	0.50	0.45	0.40	0.35	0.30
Time taken to fall (s)	3.8	3.55	3.45	3.3	2.9

1 What two forces always act on objects which fall in air?

2 Each group made a good prediction. Use the ideas of forces, gravity and air resistance to help make them even better by writing sentences of the type 'I think .... because ... .'

3 How was each test fair? What was changed, what was kept the same and what was measured changing?

4 Use the results each group recorded to plot line graphs of their findings.

5 How accurate was each test? How would you have made each test better?

Test your knowledge

1 True or false? **Five** of these ten statements are **not true**: they are false. Write down a new and accurate statement that changes each false statement into a true one.

Sir Walter Raleigh discovered gravity.

Gravity is a pulling force.

Gravity is the same size everywhere on Earth.

The Moon has a smaller gravity than the Earth.

An object's weight always stays the same.

Gravity is invisible.

All objects have gravity.

Gravity helps keep the Moon in orbit.

An object's mass always stays the same.

You would weigh less on Jupiter.

2 Write down all the words in the section 'All about forces' which have been highlighted in **bold**. Make a crossword out of these using the definitions in the Glossary, page 151, as clues. Add some related words if these will help.

3 Fill in the shaded boxes. All the words have something to do with objects falling.

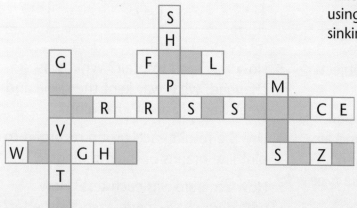

4 Sara has started to put together a map of how the ideas she has learnt in this topic all link together. Help her make her map much bigger by adding the words below and some of your own. Make it as big as you can. Use pictures if this will help.

gravity   mass   weight

air resistance   newton meter

scale   direction   size

upthrust   force diagrams

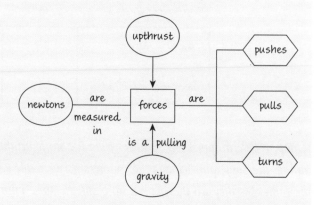

5 Draw two boats, one floating on water and on starting to sink. Show the forces, which are acting one each boat. Explain, using the idea of forces, why the boat is sinking.

How we see things

Before you start you should know that:
- there are many sources of light
- you see things with your eyes
- shadows are similar in shape to the objects that make them
- shadows are formed when light from a source is blocked
- you can see your reflection in a shiny material such as the glass in a mirror

In this unit you will learn more about how we see things and:
- that light travels in straight lines
- that we can draw diagrams of beams of light using straight lines with an arrow showing the direction in which the light is travelling
- how to draw diagrams which show how beams of light travel
- that polished surfaces reflect light better than those which are not
- that light is reflected when it hits a shiny surface
- that light sources and reflections are seen when light from them enters your eyes
- that the size of a shadow can be made larger by moving an object closer to a source of light or further away from a screen
- how to explain the difference between a shadow and a reflection

How we see things

Light is a form of energy. It always travels in straight lines. You see light sources because light from them enters your eyes. Most objects stop light getting past them. This produces shadows. When light hits the surface of an object, it is absorbed, scattered, or reflected. This allows you to see the object.

How does light travel?

A candle is a **light source**. Light travels away from the candle *in straight lines*. Some of the light shines in your eyes. This is why you see the candle.

We choose to use arrows to show where the light is going. These beams are called **light rays**.

▲ *Daniel sees a candle.*

A torch is also a light source. The torch beam shines straight out in front of you until it touches something.

- **Transparent** materials like glass allow light to travel through them perfectly.
- **Opaque** materials, such as stone, stop any light getting through at all.
- **Translucent** materials such as tracing paper let some light through.

Shadows are formed when light cannot pass through an object. Light can pass around the sides. A dark area is left behind the object. This is the **shadow**.

How do you see objects?

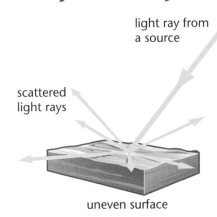

light ray from
a source

scattered
light rays

uneven surface

When a ray of light hits an object, one of the following happens:
- black surfaces absorb all the light
- other surfaces scatter the light
- very shiny surfaces reflect the light.

▲ Only a few of the light rays are drawn in this picture.

Sara is watching her cat outside at night.
- light travels outwards from the street light in all directions
- some light touches the cat
- light is scattered from the cat in all directions
- some light is scattered into Sara's eyes
- Sara sees the cat.

1 Draw a diagram to explain how you can see a light bulb. Use lines with arrows on them to show the light rays travelling from the bulb.

2 Look at the torch picture on the opposite page. Describe how the light is travelling from the torch and what is happening to it.

3 In your own words, say how shadows are formed. Draw a diagram to help you.

4 Draw and explain how the jogger sees the car. Use lines with arrows for the light rays.

Reflections

Shiny surfaces reflect light well and can produce images. An image is the 'picture' you see when you look in a mirror. Mirrors reflect light very well and make clear, sharp images. Dull surfaces reflect only a little light or none at all. You cannot see images in dull materials. Different shaped mirrors do different jobs.

Mirrors are made of a flat piece of glass, which is transparent. On the back is an extremely thin coating of silver, which is shiny. Light bounces off this very well. This is called **reflection**.

Mirrors produce extremely clear **images**. They are clear and lifelike and seem to be behind the mirror. But look carefully. The writing in the mirror looks funny. The mirror has an image in which everything appears to be the other way around to real life.

Does shape make a difference?

Most mirrors you use every day are flat. These are called plane mirrors. Some mirrors are curved. **Concave** mirrors are curved inwards, like a cave.

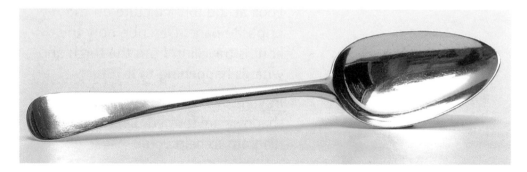

Convex mirrors are curved outwards, like the outside of a dome. A spoon is really a curved mirror. If you look at the front and back of a spoon, you will see different images.

Using mirrors every day

You can see less in a concave mirror than in a plane mirror. Objects close to a concave mirror seem bigger or magnified. Concave mirrors are often used for make-up mirrors.

You can see more of what is behind you in a convex mirror. Things look far away and smaller. Convex mirrors are used as car door mirrors.

In a plane mirror, you see a replica of your surroundings. The image appears to be the same size. This idea is used in toys like kaleidoscopes and periscopes.

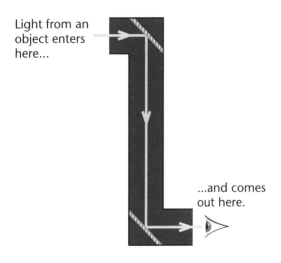

Light from an object enters here...

...and comes out here.

▲ *A periscope*

▲ *Reflective clothing is important for safety at night.*

Reflection is not simply something to have fun with. Lighthouses send warning signals by reflecting a bright light.

Torches and headlights help us see in the dark and reflective materials help us be seen at night, keeping us safe from harm.

1 What are the differences between a plane mirror, a concave mirror and a convex mirror?

2 Give an example of where you would use each of the three types of mirror.

3 Imagine that you are a ray of light. Describe your journey through a periscope. Use a diagram to help you.

4 Write a message in 'mirror writing'.

5 Which type of mirror would a dentist use to examine teeth? Why?

The size of shadows

Shadows can change in size. Moving an object near to or further away from the source of light can change the size of an object's shadow. The distance between an object and where the shadow is seen also affects the size of the shadow.

Planning an investigation

Mr Smith has set his class the problem of investigating what affects the size of a shadow. Jack and Tom have come up with the following ideas and plans.

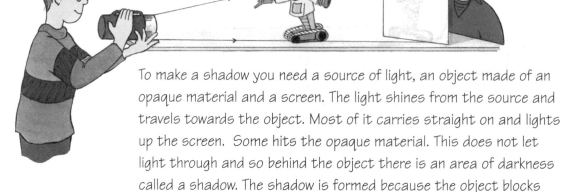

To make a shadow you need a source of light, an object made of an opaque material and a screen. The light shines from the source and travels towards the object. Most of it carries straight on and lights up the screen. Some hits the opaque material. This does not let light through and so behind the object there is an area of darkness called a shadow. The shadow is formed because the object blocks some of the light travelling towards the screen.

We are going to look at how changing the distance between the object and the screen and the distance between the torch and the object has on the size of the shadow.

Jack made an object out of cardboard and used a torch as a source of light. I have found a screen to form the shadows on. We will need to switch off all the lights and cover the windows with paper to block out most of the sunlight.

	What we keep the same	What we will change	What we will measure
Test 1	Distance between the object and the screen: the angle which the torch shines on the object	Distance between the torch (light source) and the object	The size of the shadows every time we move the torch closer to the object
Test 2	Distance between the torch and the object: the angle which the torch shines on the object	Distance between the object and the screen	The size of the shadows every time we move the object closer to the screen

Carrying out the investigation

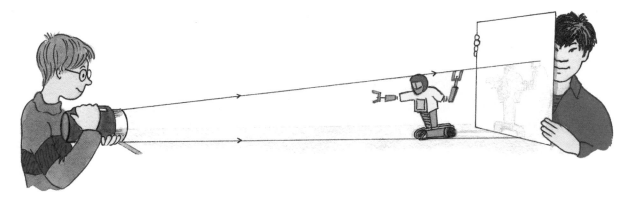

Test 1

Here are the results we recorded when we changed the distance between the torch and the object.

Distance between the torch and the object (cm)	20	40	60	80	100
Size of the shadow (cm)	95	50	31	24	20

Test 2

Here are the results we recorded when we changed the distance between the object and the screen.

Distance between the object and screen (m)	1.0	1.25	1.5	1.75	2.0
Size of the shadow (cm)	10	13	15	17	21

1 Write down sentences that explain what the following words mean:

shadow opaque source

2 How did Jack and Tom make their tests fair?

3 Why did they repeat some measurements?

4 Record their results in line graphs. Label your graphs correctly.

5 What did Jack and Tom find out about the factors which help change the size of shadows?

The difference between shadows and reflections

Shadows and reflections look completely different. Shadows are formed on opaque surfaces and you can only see an object's shape in dark outline. Reflections are formed on shiny surfaces and you can see an image of the object just like it is in real life. Shadows and reflections can be explained by how light travels.

Looking at a reflection

Sara looked at her reflection in a mirror

I can see my reflection in a mirror because it has a very smooth, shiny surface. Dull surfaces do not make good mirrors.

My reflection looks just like me in real life. I can see every detail in my face, in full colour. But if I put one finger to my right eye it looks as if my reflection has put her finger to her left eye. So it is not quite the same. My reflection also looks as if she is as far behind the mirror as I am in front and is the right way up.

Looking at a shadow

Sara then looked at her shadow.

I cannot see my shadow on shiny objects like mirrors. Shadows are best formed on dull surfaces.

My shadow only shows my outline. I can only see my shape. My shadow is dark and I cannot see any detail. If I put my finger to my right ear it looks as if my shadow has put her finger to her left ear. My shadow looks as if it is lying on the ground.

How can you explain the differences?

Before she can explain the differences Sara has to understand some key ideas.

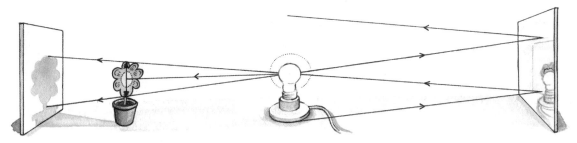

Shadows are made when light is blocked by an opaque surface.

Light travels in straight lines from a source.

Light is reflected and changes direction when it hits a shiny surface.

My shadow is dark and surrounded by a brightly lit up area. Some light from the lamp hits me and is stopped by my opaque surface. Light, which hits either side of me carries on and lights up the screen. I see a shadow because the bright light from the screen is reflected back into my eyes. The dark area has no light that can travel back.

My finger is reflected in the mirror. I can see this because light that has bounced off my finger has travelled to the mirror. When it hits the mirror it is reflected, and some of the light travels into my eye. Other light rays bounce off from different parts of my finger. When they are reflected into my eye a picture of my whole finger builds up and this is what I see.

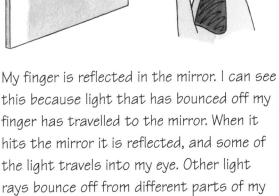

1 What surfaces produce shadows and reflections?

2 Write down three ways in which a shadow and a reflection are different.

3 Use your knowledge of how light moves to explain why there are these differences between shadows and reflections.

HOW WE SEE THINGS

Test your knowledge

1 Make a word search containing all of these words or phrases. Make it bigger by adding some words of your own about how we see light.

image	light source	energy
light rays	reflect	absorb
shiny	opaque	scatter
shadow	dark	dull

2 Write a story which includes all the shadows and reflections you might see in a typical day.

3 All of the following sentences are **false**; they are not true. Re-write them without the mistakes to make them true sentences.

Light travels in circles.

Opaque materials let light through them.

A shadow is formed when light passes through a shiny surface.

Mirrors are made of a translucent material which absorbs light.

Real light rays have arrows written on them.

4 Use the library to find out the answers to the following questions.

a   How fast does light travel?

b   How do you make a mirror?

c   Where are periscopes used?

5 Explain what is happening in this picture.

6 Explain what is happening in this picture.

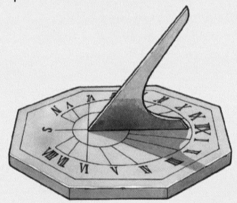

7 Make drawings to show how:

a   you see your friend's nose

b   your shadow is formed on the playground

c   how you see your face in the mirror.

132

Electrical circuits

Before you start you should know that:

- circuits will only work if they are complete
- switches can be used to control devices in a circuit
- metals are good conductors of electricity
- plastics are poor conductors of electricity and good electrical insulators

In this unit you will learn more about electrical circuits and that:

- each component in a circuit can be drawn using a special symbol
- there are agreed ways of drawing a circuit and the correct symbols have to be used
- if you see a circuit you should be able to draw it using the correct symbols
- the brightness of bulbs or the speed of motors in a circuit can be changed
- if you overload a circuit it will burn out
- wires are usually covered in plastic because it is an electrical insulator

Drawing circuits

Electrical components can be drawn using a set of symbols. Each component has its own symbol. There are agreed ways of drawing them in a circuit. Sometimes it matters which way round a component is connected. Symbols have to be able to show which way round the components are connected.

Michelle wanted to draw her **circuits** in her book. She didn't want to spend ages drawing each component. There are some agreed symbols that she should use instead.

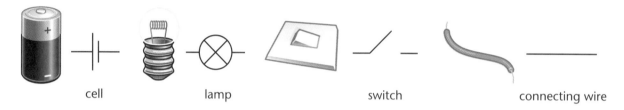

cell   lamp   switch   connecting wire

When drawing the circuits she does not need to show the connecting wires as the right shape or length. She only has to show how they are connected together. They are often drawn as straight lines because that looks neater.

Michelle made a circuit. She used a **cell**, three connecting wires, a **switch** and a lamp. She put them in a complete circuit with the switch to control the flow. She then drew it in her book using the symbols.

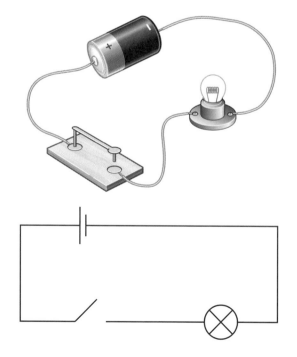

Using symbols helps you draw a *plan* of the circuit. The route around the circuit for the current to flow is shown. It also shows how the components are linked together. Switches are *always* drawn open.

The right way round

Michelle needs to show which way round her cell or cells are connected. A cell has a + sign at one **terminal** and a – sign at the other. The long vertical line on the symbol is the positive (+) side and the shorter line is the negative (–).

Several cells together are called a **battery**. Michelle can link the symbols for individual cells together to show a battery. Just like a single cell, the symbol for a battery has to show which terminal is which.

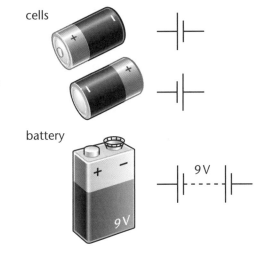

cells

battery

Some other components

Michelle will not only want to draw circuits with cells and lamps. Her circuits may include some other components. She will need to know what symbols have been agreed for them.

A **motor** will spin when the current flows. A **buzzer** will vibrate and make a sound. If an **LED** is put in the right way round it will light up like a tiny lamp as the current flows through it. A **resistor** is any component that makes it difficult for the current to flow.

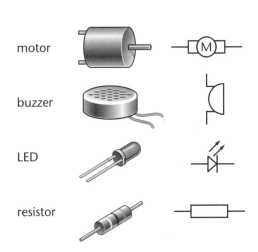

motor

buzzer

LED

resistor

1 Here is a diagram of a torch. Draw its circuit using the agreed symbols.

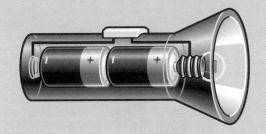

2 Draw a circuit diagram to show a motor and a lamp controlled by a single switch.

3 Here are some circuits drawn in symbols. Describe the circuits in words. The first has been done for you.

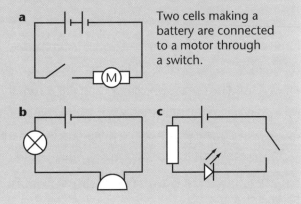

a   Two cells making a battery are connected to a motor through a switch.

b

c

Making motors go faster

Many circuits contain an electrical motor. You can change the speed of motor in a circuit in a number of ways. If batteries power the circuit you could change the number or voltage of batteries you use. Adding more batteries or using higher voltage batteries will make the motor go faster.

Changing the speed of motors in a circuit

Jamal did some experiments to find out how she could speed up electrical motors.

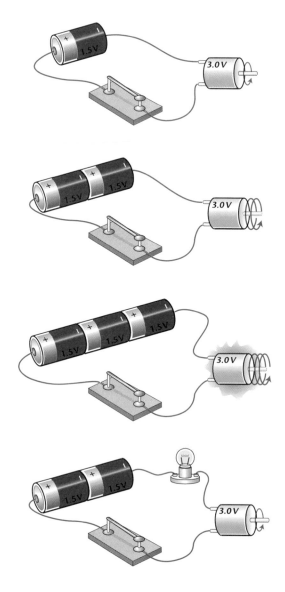

Here is my first circuit. It only has a one 1.5 V battery, a motor, connecting wires and a switch. The motor has 3.0 V written on the side. I think this means that it is meant to work with a 3.0 V battery. The circuit works well but the motor only turns round slowly.

Next I added a second 1.5 V battery into the circuit. The two batteries give a total voltage of 3.0 V. I thought the motor would turn around at a steady speed and it did.

I wondered what would happen if a third battery was added. It was a bad idea. The motor turned around much quicker as I thought, but got very hot, made a smell and stopped working. The circuit was overloaded and the motor burnt out. The 3.0 V motor is not designed to work with higher voltages than this.

Finally I made a circuit with two 1.5 V batteries, a 3.0 V motor and a 1.5 V lamp. The motor turned slowly and the lamp was dim. I thought carefully what was going on. The batteries were supplying a total of 3.0 V and the motor and the lamp needed a total of 4.5 V to make them work normally. They would only work well if I added an extra battery to supply 4.5 V to the circuit.

Drawing circuits correctly

Jamal then drew the circuits she had made. She had seen some circuits drawn with the wrong symbols so she found out which were the correct ones.

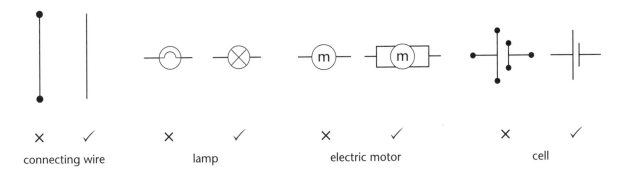

Then she drew the circuits. She made sure there was a complete circuit in each one and that she used the correct symbols. Usually the diagrams are started with the cells or batteries at the top.

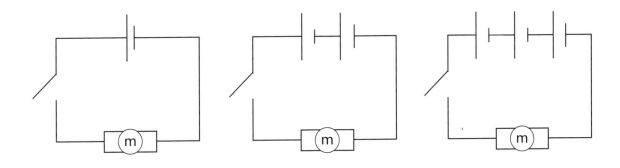

A complete circuit with a 1.5 V cell, a 3.0 V motor and a switch. The motor turns slowly.

A complete circuit with two 1.5 V cells, a 3.0 V motor and switch. The motor turns normally.

A complete circuit with three 1.5 V cells, a 3.0 V motor and switch. The motor burns out.

1 Name three ways in which you could make a motor in a circuit turn faster.

2 What happens when you overload a circuit?

3 Jamal has not yet drawn her final circuit with two 1.5 V cells, a motor and a lamp. Can you draw it?

Brighter lamps and dimmer lamps

The brightness of a lamp in a circuit depends on the size of the current flowing through it. The current can be changed by changing the number of components that it has to flow through, the voltage of the cell or cells that drives it around and the paths that are available for it to take.

Tom had a lamp connected through a switch to a cell.

He added a second lamp...

...and then a third lamp.

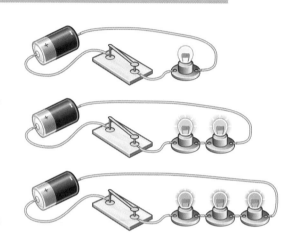

When he switched on he found that each additional lamp made all the lamps dimmer.

The brightness of the lamps depends on the size of the current flowing. Each lamp makes it harder for the current to flow and the size of the current gets smaller.
The lamps act as electrical **resistors**. If we put too many lamps in the circuit the current will not be big enough to light them.

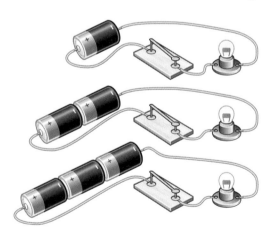

Tom then tried adding more cells with his single lamp in the circuit. He was careful to add the cells the same way around, with the + terminal of one joined to the – terminal of the next.

He tried two cells...

...and then a third cell.

He found that adding more cells made the lamp brighter.

The cells provide the **voltage** that drives the current around the circuit. Adding cells makes the voltage bigger. A bigger voltage can drive a bigger current and the lamp will be brighter. If the voltage is too high for the lamp, the wire inside it will glow so brightly that it will melt. This will break the circuit and the lamp will go off.

Trying to get something for nothing

Tom took a single cell and three lamps. He connected his lamps so that they were in a single line in a circuit. We call this arrangement a **series** circuit. The lamps were very dim.

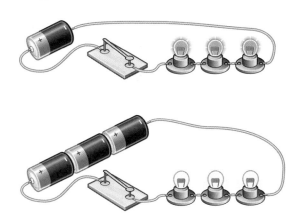

He needed three cells to drive the current to get his lamps to light as brightly as a single lamp connected to a single cell. Three cells would give enough voltage for three lamps.

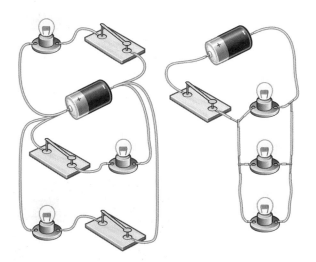

Michelle only had one cell but she wanted to have three lamps brightly lit. She connected each lamp in its own circuit across her cell. Each lamp was brightly lit.

She then connected them in separate branches of the same circuit. Again they were all brightly lit.

These circuits are called **parallel** circuits. They give the current a choice of route around the circuit.

Each lamp has enough voltage to light it brightly.

Unfortunately for Michelle her cell will not last very long. It is having to do a lot of work keeping all three lamps brightly lit.

1 Put the lamps in these circuits in order of brightness starting with the brightest.

2 Which lamp will be lit for the longest time? Explain your choice.

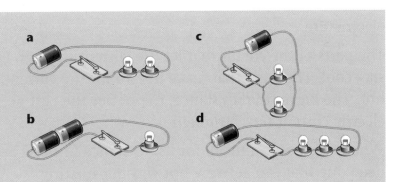

Some useful electrical appliances

Two important electrical properties are the magnetic effect of an electric current and the heating effect when an electrical current flows. We can use these properties in electrical appliances. The properties decide how the appliance behaves in an electrical circuit and what we can use it for.

An electric motor

A motor uses the **magnetic effect** of an electric current to cause a coil of wire to spin when a current flows through it.

Many **appliances** that you use at home contain electric motors. These include food mixers, drills, vacuum cleaners, washing machines and tumble dryers.

The speed of the motor depends on the current flowing through it. A bigger current means a faster spin.

Some motors will spin clockwise when the current flows one way and anticlockwise when it flows the other way.

▲ *Motor of a washing machine.*

Heating coils

When a current flows in a circuit it makes the circuit hot. This is the **heating effect** of an electric current. The harder it is for the current to flow, the hotter the circuit gets.

A lamp glows because the filament inside it makes it hard for the current to flow. It is an electrical **resistor**. This **resistance** makes the filament in the lamp hot.

We use the same idea in an electric kettle, a toaster or an electric fire.

▲ *A filament glowing in a lamp.*

The parts of the circuit that let the current through easily stay cool. The parts that make it hard for the current to flow get hot. The bigger the resistance, the hotter the part gets when an electric current flows through it.

When we choose a metal for its resistance in these appliances we need one that can get very hot without melting.

A light-emitting diode

Light-emitting diodes are often just called **LEDs** from the initial letters of their name. They give out *light* when a current flows through them.

Sara wanted to put one in a circuit. She found that it mattered which way round she connected it into her circuit. When it was the right way round it glowed brightly. When it was connected the wrong way round it didn't glow.

The right way round they are **conductors**, but the wrong way makes them **insulators**.

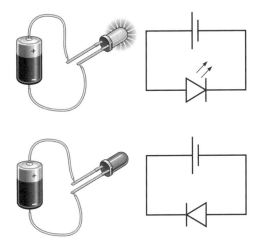

A buzzer

A **buzzer** vibrates when a current passes through it.

The bigger the current, the bigger the vibration it causes. This makes the buzz louder.

Some buzzers will only work if the current flows through them in the right direction. They need to be connected into the circuit the right way round.

1 Write down four appliances found in many homes that have an electric motor in them.

2 A model is powered by a motor. Here is a diagram of the circuit. Redraw the circuit so that the motor will spin the other way.

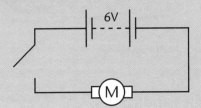

3 Here is a diagram of a circuit that Mina set up. The LED was meant to glow to let her know when the motor was on. When she closed the switch, nothing happened. All the components were all right. What could be wrong? Redraw the circuit to put it right.

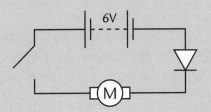

Electrical safety

High voltages can kill. Mains voltage is 240 volts. Electrical conductors need to be kept away from electrical appliances. Water reduces the electrical resistance of your body and this makes bathrooms hazardous. Damaged cables can be very dangerous. Overheating in circuits can and should be avoided.

People know that an electric shock can hurt or even kill them. For a shock to happen we need a high voltage. Voltages of over 25 volts are high. When we use mains electricity, at home or at school, we are using a voltage of about 240 volts.

To get a shock, two parts of your body need to be connected to conductors. One of the conductors has to be at a high voltage. Never put metal objects into electrical appliances or sockets as this can make you part of a high voltage circuit.

Mina has got her toast stuck in the toaster. She knows it is very silly to try to free it with cutlery. She must switch off and unplug it first.

Electricity and water

It is easy to forget that tap water is a conductor and that water on your skin will make you a better conductor. This is why bathrooms have special precautions to make them safe to use.

Never take portable electrical appliances into a bathroom. You might get an electric shock. Only shavers should be plugged into their own special sockets.

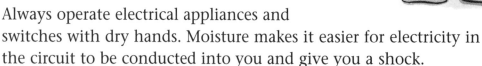

Always operate electrical appliances and switches with dry hands. Moisture makes it easier for electricity in the circuit to be conducted into you and give you a shock.

To be safe, *keep water away* from mains electric switches and cables.

Damaged cables

The conducting part of an electrical cable is covered with an insulator to protect you. It stops you from coming into contact with the electrical circuit.

Damage to the insulator can make it easier for you to touch the metal conductor inside. Do not use an appliance with frayed cables. Get someone to replace them before you use it.

Jack's father is using a soldering iron. He needs to be very careful not to melt the insulating cover. Then he would be able to touch the circuit.

You need to be careful whenever you use a hot appliance.

Fire dangers in electrical circuits

Electrical currents cause the conductors that they flow through to heat up. If the current is too big, the heating can cause burns or a fire.

It is best not to put many plugs in one socket as this can cause it to heat up. Use just *one* plug in *one* socket or use a proper **adaptor**.

Never plug other appliances into lamp sockets as this too can cause a fire.

Always stop using an appliance if you see smoke or sparks, or if it makes a strange noise.

1 Explain why you should not stick a knife or fork into a toaster while it is still plugged in.

2 Explain why bathrooms have pull-cord switches.

3 When should you use a proper adaptor?

4 What is the job of the covering on an electric cable?

5 Explain why you should never balance a television on the side of a bath.

6 What signs might there be to suggest something is wrong with an appliance?

Test your knowledge

1 The circuits below have had their wires jumbled together. To which end, P, Q, R, S or T, should the lead from the battery be joined to:

   a sound the buzzer?

   b light the lamp?

   c work the motor?

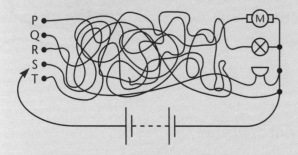

2 On your own copy of the word spiral fill in the words that answer these clues. The letter at the end of one word is the starting letter of the next.

  1 A controlled break in a circuit.

  2 What conductors get as a current forces its way through them.

  3 The end of a cell or battery.

  4 A device that glows when a current flows through it.

  5 The object that joins an appliance to a mains circuit.

  6 An unusual non-metallic material.

  7 A very useful type of energy.

3 Imagine your life with no electricity. Write an account of a typical day explaining how you managed to do all the usual things that normally rely on electricity, such as making a cup of coffee for breakfast or listening to music on the radio.

4 Three electrical units, the ampere, the volt and the ohm, are named after three famous scientists: André Ampère, Alessandro Volta and Georg Ohm.

Find out when they lived, where they lived, what they did and any other interesting facts about their lives and ideas.

5 You know that electricity can be dangerous. Design and make a poster to warn young children of some of the dangers of working with or near electricity.

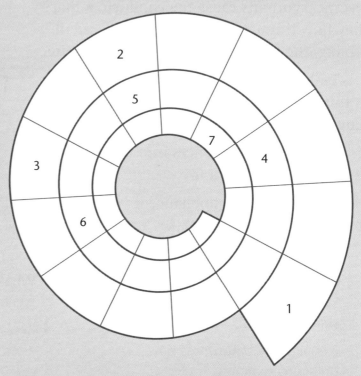

Glossary

Keeping healthy

Alcoholic   A person who is addicted to alcohol. Being an alcoholic can cause serious damage to the body.

Artery   A blood vessel going away from the heart taking blood which is rich in oxygen.

Bacteria   Micro-organisms which can cause diseases. Only some bacteria are harmful; many are useful.

Body organ   Part of the body which does a particular job. The eyes, heart, brain, ears, skin, lungs, heart and kidneys are all organs.

Brain   This controls all of your senses, muscles and organs in your body.

Diet   What we eat and drink.

Digestive system   This system is made up of many different organs which digest food and absorb its goodness into your body.

Drug addiction   When someone cannot stop taking harmful drugs, such as alcohol, heroin, nicotine or cocaine.

Energy   You use this when you do work like climbing the stairs, lifting a bag or play a game. You also need it for growing.

Fibre   This is found in fruit and vegetables and is needed to keep our intestines working properly.

Fungi   Only some of these micro-organisms cause diseases like athlete's foot.

Heart   This pumps blood around your body. It is found in your chest and is about the size of a fist. It is made of strong muscle.

Micro-organisms   Very small living organisms, such as bacteria, that can only be seen with a microscope.

Muscles   Muscles carry out all of the body's movements. You have more than 600 muscles which accounts for about half of your body weight.

Nerves   These connect your brain to the rest of your body and allow you to feel, see, hear, taste and smell. Nerves are also connected to your muscles and control how you move.

Pulse rate   The number of times the heart beats in one minute. A human heart beats about 30 million times a year and 2 billion times in a lifetime.

Reproduction   To make more of something. Animals reproduce by having babies. This is called sexual reproduction.

Scurvy   A diseases caused by lack of vitamin C in our diet.

Skeleton   The bones which support your body. The average person has 206 bones.

Vein   A blood vessel going to the heart taking blood which is less rich in oxygen.

Viruses   These cause diseases and are so small that they cannot be seen under an ordinary microscope.

Living together

Adaptation The way in which plants and animals are suited to their particular habitat.

Carnivore An animal that eats the meat of another animal.

Carpel Part of a flower. Each is made of an ovary, style and stigma.

Chlorophyll The green pigment in leaves which helps the plant make food.

Consumers Animals are all consumers because they eat plants or other animals.

Decay The breakdown of material due to micro-organisms.

Fertilisation When part of the pollen tube joins with part of the ovule.

Food chain A diagram showing who eats what. It starts with a plant which is eaten by an animal, which is eaten by another animal, and so on.

Fruit The hard or fleshy part of a plant that makes a container for the seeds. It is made from the wall of the ovary.

Germination When a seed starts to grow and produces a small root and shoot.

Habitat The place or environment where particular plants and animals live.

Herbivores Animals that eat plants.

Key This is used to place things into their correct groups or to identify them.

Life cycle Young plants and animals grow up and then reproduce. These young then continue the same cycle.

Nutrients Mineral salts dissolved in soil water which are needed for plant growth.

Ovary The part of the carpel where the ovules are produced.

Ovule The part of the carpel which becomes the seed when it has been fertilised.

Petal The part of the flower which is usually brightly coloured.

Photosynthesis The process that plants use to make their own food from carbon dioxide and water using light.

Pollen Small grains which are produced at the top of the stamen. These are needed to fertilise ovules.

Pollination The transfer of pollen from the stamens of one flower to the stigma of another flower of the same type.

Producers Plants are called producers because they use energy from the Sun to make their own food.

Seeds After fertilisation, the ovules become seeds. These can grow to form new plants.

Sepal Part of the flower which protects it as it grows.

Stamen Part of the flower where pollen is made. Pollen grains are carried by insects or wind to other flowers of the same type.

Stigma Top part of the carpel which pollen grains stick to.

Style Part of the carpel which joins the stigma to the ovary. Pollen tubes grow down this to fertilise the ovules.

Gases and changing states

Carbon dioxide   A common gas which you make in your body when you make energy. It is also found dissolved in fizzy drinks. It has no taste and is colourless.

Condensation   The change which occurs when a gas cools and turns into a liquid. An example is water vapour condensing on a cold surface to form liquid water.

Evaporation   The change which occurs when a liquid is heated and turns into a gas. Puddles of water evaporate on a warm day to form water vapour.

Freezing   The change which happens when a liquid cools and turns into a solid. An example is when liquid water turns into solid ice when you put it in the freezer.

Gap   An unfilled space. Materials have gaps between their particles.

Gas   One of the three states of matter. Any air-like substance which moves freely to fill any space available.

Helium   A rare gas which is lighter than air. It is used in balloons to make them rise and in special light bulbs where it makes them light up in a special colour.

Liquid   One of the three states of matter. Liquids like water can flow and take up the shape of any container they are put in.

Melting   The change which happens when a solid is heated and turns into a liquid. An example is solid ice turning into liquid water. Melting is not the same as dissolving.

Nitrogen   The gas that forms the main part of the air. It is clear, colourless and odourless.

Oxygen   A common gas found in the air. You breath this in and it is used in your body to help keep you alive.

Saturated   When all the spaces in something are filled up and it can take no more in.

Solid   One of the three states of matter. Any materials which is a solid is usually hard and has a shape which can only be changed if you hit it hard.

State   Whether a material is a solid, a liquid or a gas.

Water cycle   A natural cycle of events in which water moves through the environment changing from solid to liquid to gas as it does so.

Water vapour   The name given to the gas form of water.

Changes in materials

Aluminium sulphate   Name of a chemical used at water treatment works to help clump small insoluble solids together so that they can be removed by filtering.

Burning   A chemical change that is irreversible. New materials are always made in this process. Materials cannot burn without oxygen.

Chemical change   An irreversible change that makes new materials.

Chlorine   A chemical used to kill microbes in water that is being cleaned for drinking.

Dissolve   The name given to the change when a solid passes into a solution.

Impurities   A pure substance which is contaminated with another material.

Insoluble   The name given to a solid that will not dissolve. For example, sand does not dissolve in water.

Irreversible change   A change made to a material that cannot be reversed. Burning paper is an example of an irreversible change. When paper burns it makes ash, carbon dioxide and water. You cannot get the paper back once it has burnt.

Mixture   A material which has two or more chemical substances which are not chemically joined to each other.

Particles   Small pieces of a material. You can see small particles with your eyes. But if you really magnify a material the smallest particles are very, very small. They cannot even be seen with a normal microscope.

Reversible change   A change made to a material that can easily be reversed. Melting, freezing, evaporating and condensing are all examples of reversible changes. These things happen naturally all of the time.

Saturated   The state reached when a solution will not dissolve any more material.

Soluble   The name given to a solid that dissolves. Some solids that will not dissolve in water may dissolve in other liquids. For example, biro ink will not dissolve in water but will dissolve in another liquid called propanone.

Solute   The name given to a dissolved substance. For example, when salt is dissolved in water, salt is a solute.

Solution   A liquid that has another substance dissolved in it.

Solvent   The name given to the liquid part of a solution. Water is a very common solvent.

Stirring   This speeds up the process of dissolving but does not increase the total amount of solute that can dissolve.

Water vapour   The name given to the gas form of water.

Our Earth and the solar system

Axis   An imaginary line passing through the North and South poles of the Earth. The Earth spins on this axis.

Crescent   The curved shape of the Moon which you see when only a small amount (less than half) of it is lit up in the sky by the Sun.

Day   The time it takes for the Earth to spin once on its axis. This takes 24 hours. The length of a day is different on other planets.

Daytime   The time of the day when your part of the Earth is facing towards the Sun and it is light.

Equinox   The two times in the year when the length of daylight is equal to the length of darkness.

Lunar eclipse   When the Moon, Sun and Earth are lined up in space so that the Earth casts a shadow on the Moon.

Lunar month   The time taken for our Moon to make one complete orbit around the Earth. The time taken to do this is just over 28 days.

Moon   A large object which orbits a planet. The Earth has one moon orbiting it. At the last count there were 46 moons around the planets in our solar system.

Night or **Night-time**   The time of the day when your part of the Earth is facing away from the Sun and you are in darkness.

Orbit   The path taken when a planet moves around a star or a moon around a planet. Most planets move in almost circular orbits.

Phases of the Moon   The changing shape of the Moon at different times of the month. The amount which is lit up that we can see depends upon the Moon's position in its orbit.

Planet   Planets are smaller than stars and are not sources of light or heat. Planets can be seen because they reflect light.

Rotation   The turning of an object, such as the Earth, on its axis.

Season   The name given to a period during each year when there is a change in length of daylight, such as spring, summer, autumn and winter.

Solar eclipse   When the Moon passes exactly between the Earth and the Sun and casts a shadow on the Earth.

Solar system   A group of large objects anywhere in space which has a star with orbiting planets. Our solar system has the Sun and nine planets.

Solstice   The two times in the year when the length of daylight is either at its longest or its shortest.

Star   Massive objects in the universe which release their own energy through nuclear reactions. The Sun is our nearest star.

Changing sounds

Amplitude   The size of a vibration or the height of the peaks and troughs of a wave.

Ear drum   This transmits vibrations from the outer ear to the small bones in the middle ear.

Frequency   The number of times a wave vibrates in one second.

Insulators   Materials which can prevent sound from travelling.

Oscilloscope   A device which can be used to show sounds as moving waves on a screen. The amplitude and frequency can then be measured.

Pitch   How high or low a sound seems. Fast, high frequency vibrations give high notes. Slow, low frequency vibrations give low notes.

Sound source   Something that makes a sound when it vibrates.

Sound waves   The vibrations made by a sound source. Pulses of sound energy.

Vibration   Rapid movement backwards and forwards around a fixed point.

Wave   A regular vibration in a material. Waves carry energy. The bigger the amplitude of the wave, the greater the amount of energy.

Wavelength   The length of one vibration of a wave.

All about forces

Air resistance The name given to the friction force which is caused when an object moves through the air. It tries to stop or slow down the object from moving.

Calibrate When you mark out a scale on a measuring instrument.

Force A push, pull, a twist or a turn. Gravity, friction, air and water resistance are all examples of forces. The units of force are newtons (N).

Force diagram A diagram which shows how forces act on an object. It has arrows which show the size and direction of each force.

Friction The name given to the force that occurs when two objects move over each other.

Gravity The name of an attractive force that acts on all objects on the Earth. It pulls the objects towards the centre of the Earth. Gravity also acts on other planets and very large objects.

Mass The name given to the amount of material in an object. An object's mass is always the same. It is measured in grams.

Newton(s) The unit of force. It is named after the English scientist Sir Isaac Newton who was the first person to put together ideas about forces.

Newton meter or **force meter** An instrument which measures the size of forces. It contains a strong spring which alters its length as more force is applied.

Scale The markings on the side of a scientific instrument that help you work out the size of what you are measuring.

Upthrust A force exerted by water on an object which pushes upwards.

Water resistance The name given to the friction force which is caused when an object moves through water. Just like air resistance, it tries to stop or slow down the object from moving.

Weight The name given to the size of the force of gravity which is acting on an object's mass. The bigger the mass, the bigger is the object's weight.

How we see things

Image The 'picture' of the world seen in a mirror or made by a lens.

Light rays The beams of light which come from a light source.

Light source Something which makes its own light, like a candle or the Sun.

Mirror Any smooth, shiny surface which reflects light perfectly.

Opaque Materials which do not let light pass through them, like wood.

Reflection This happens when light is bounced off a material. If the surface is flat and shiny, like a mirror, a clear image of the object can be seen.

Shadow The dark area formed when an object blocks some of the light which is falling on it.

Translucent Materials which allow only some light to pass through them, like tracing paper.

Transparent Materials which allow light to travel through them perfectly. Glass is used for windows because it is transparent.

Electrical circuits

Appliance A device or component used for a special purpose. An electric fire is an appliance used to heat a room.

Battery Two or more cells joined together. When joined in series they make the voltage bigger. When joined in parallel they last longer.

Buzzer A device that changes electrical energy into sound. When a current flows through it, it vibrates.

Cell A device that changes chemical into electrical energy. It has a positive (+) and a negative (–) terminal for connection to the circuit.

Circuit A closed loop that lets the current flow round. The circuit starts and ends with the cell or battery.

Conductor A material that allows an electric current to flow through it. All metals are conductors.

Current A flow of electricity around a circuit. This flow allows appliances to work. It also causes heating and magnetic effects.

Graphite A form of carbon. It is unusual in that it is a non-metal that allows a current through it. It is a non-metallic conductor.

Heating effect The rise in temperature found in a conductor whenever a current flows through it.

Insulator A material that does not allow the flow of an electrical current through it. Most non-metals are insulators.

LED A light-emitting diode. This glows when a current flows through it. It will only allow a flow of current in one direction.

Magnetic effect The making of a magnet whenever a current flows through a conductor.

Motor A device that changes electrical energy into movement. When a current flows through it, it spins.

Parallel A circuit in which the components are connected to each other so that the current has a choice of routes.

Resistance The force in an electrical conductor which makes it difficult for a current to flow.

Resistor A conductor that makes it difficult for the current to flow in the circuit. The bigger the resistance the smaller the current.

Series A circuit in which the components are connected to each other so that a current has to flow through all of them before it gets back to the cell.

Switch A break in a circuit that can be controlled. The current flows when the switch is closed and stops when the switch is open.

Terminal The end of a cell or battery that is used to connect it to the rest of the circuit. Each cell has a positive (+) and a negative (–) terminal.

Voltage The amount of electrical push that drives the current around the circuit. The bigger the voltage, the bigger the current.

Index